WITHDRAW

ART AND CONCEPT

LUCIAN KRUKOWSKI

Art and Concept

A PHILOSOPHICAL STUDY

THE UNIVERSITY OF MASSACHUSETTS PRESS

AMHERST

1987

Copyright © 1987 by The University of Massachusetts Press
All rights reserved
Printed in the United States of America
Set in Linoterm Aldus at The University of Massachusetts Press
Printed by Cushing-Malloy and bound by John Dekker & Sons

Library of Congress Cataloging-in-Publication Data

Krukowski, Lucian, 1929–
    Art and concept.
    Includes index.
    1. Aesthetics. I. Title.
BH39.K69   1987   701   87–5012
ISBN 0–87023–563–x (alk. paper)

British Library Cataloguing in Publication Data are available.

88003835

To My Wife and Daughter

CONTENTS

PREFACE

The origins of this book can be traced to a time when writing one would have seemed an absurd idea—even as a projection for my distant middle age. It was the time when I slowed my sophomoric drift by deciding not to join the merchant marine and, instead, became an art student. The circumstances of my study were quite adventitious; they included being born in Brooklyn and attending the city university. As it also turned out, among my teachers were important figures in the then-burgeoning New York School of American painting: Ad Reinhardt, Burgoyne Diller, Mark Rothko, and Harry Holtzman. They were the first, really, to show me what a wider world could be like, and I want here to indicate my debt to them. These artists were not at ease with the then-standard connotations of "teacher": Having anticipated Rorty by some decades, they opted, in their own teaching, for good conversation over studio procedures. Not that we didn't make "things," you understand, but there seemed no point to the making unless it was found in what was said. And, as much was being said, the things that were made gained, lost, and traded their artistic identities in the course of the conversations. We did not take what was said as merely "explanation" or "justification"; it seemed more central, to be taken, rather, as a proper part of what we identified as a work. Thus, the juncture of "art and concept" was among my first experiences of art. How this juncture actually occurs seemed clear and unproblematic to me then; that it is not so now is one reason for this book.

I remember that one of the consequences of this way of teaching was the "dignity" the evoked concepts gave to all our efforts—from the casual to the ambitious. The fact that, retrospectively, such dignity was often misplaced seems unimportant now. Actually, there were few histrionics involved in the situation, for there was little audience. What mattered was that, in this way, we students were effectively shielded from the notion of accumulated skills and, thus, from any residue of academic training or, even, from procedures of the European atelier. So we were, from the beginning, "artists" not "students"; our youthful limitations seemed to have no necessary relation to the value of what we produced, for the things took on their own identities as they were entered into the realm of conversation. I now see this as an early variant of the more recent attempts to liberate artists and their works from each other.

Some years later, I came to better understand the perils of this formalized precociousness. I was drafted and spent time on a military rifle range in North Carolina. My days were filled with noise and repetitive duties, but in the late afternoons I was often able to return to the ranges, then still and empty, to continue my imprimatur of "making art." It was quite lovely, really, with the expanses of grass, a few low buildings, and the birds—well used to the routine—that would appear at dusk when the shooting was over. I came there with my small bundle of supplies and, sitting on the grass, doggedly made my abstractions. The "concepts" in question were more fickle by then—having lost the communal stability that school provides—and so my art became many things, varying from day to day, even moment to moment. I passed the time devising scenarios my objects could partake in, and found that each member of each pair I devised—object and scenario—could be interchanged, even if the plausibility of certain pairings required more effort to sustain than did others.

This was a freedom that, even if exquisitely clear and pristine, verged on emptiness; it was too frightening, and I was glad to return to New York where I entered into the usual course of painting, showing, and teaching. But the regained comforts of the "artworld" diffused the pointedness—and point—of this earlier experience, and it was not until much later that I again faced these issues in a more direct way.

After some years, I moved to Washington University in St. Louis to teach art and administrate, and—although it was not part of the agreement—to become a student again, this time in philosophy. It so happened that in the course of some early social gatherings I met the philosopher Richard Rudner —who was also a great conversationalist and who, after a time, gently suggested that I take a few courses so that my own rhetoric might be leavened with some rigor. The few became many and, to the general bemusement, I eventually received my degree, with Rudner chairing my dissertation. I would like here to acknowledge my debt to him. As I was also painting and showing at this time, I count it as a later instantiation of "art and concept."

The problems I take up in this book, then, come out of my efforts as an artist and a philosopher. This stance, however, while it may identify a basis and reason for theorizing, carries no inherent value claims. I do not take my history to be a proper part of my work, nor do I take my dual activities as imparting a special value to each other simply through their propinquity. Whatever value any of these works may have is the discrete concern of the viewer or, as in this case, the reader.

Although some of the chapters in this book are based upon earlier published articles, they have all been revised in the light of new material. However, I am happy to acknowledge the publications in which these earlier versions occur. They are: chapter 1, "Hegel, 'Progress' and the Avant-Garde; A Study in the Visual Arts," in *Journal of Aesthetics and Art Criticism* 44, no. 3 (Spring 1986); chapter 3, "Form and Protest in Atonal Music: A Meditation on Adorno," in *Bucknell Review*, ed. Harry Garvin, 29, no. 1, Bucknell University Press (1984); chapter 4, " 'Appreciation,' 'Obligation,' and an Artwork's End," in *Journal of Aesthetic Education* 17, no. 2 (Summer 1983), © 1983 Board of Trustees of the University of Illinois; chapter 5, "Artworks That End and Objects That Endure," *Journal of Aesthetics and Art Criticism* 40, no. 2 (Winter 1981); and chapter 6, "A Basis for Attributions of 'Art,' " *Journal of Aesthetics and Art Criticism* 39, no. 1 (Fall 1980).

There are many who have shared different parts of my life and thus, however indirectly, have contributed to this book. They are old friends, loves, colleagues, and students, and I would like to remember them here. But time has passed and so that none may be slighted I will not name any individually, but I do send my greetings to them all.

ART AND CONCEPT

INTRODUCTION

This book is on the relationship between certain theories or "concepts" about art and particular periods or "styles" in art. The concepts by and large come from philosophy, and the art is mostly located in that part of modernism known as the "avant-garde." My arrays of art and concepts are not always chronologically parallel: In chapters 1 and 2, the artworks I discuss are of the twentieth century whereas the conceptual sources reach back to the eighteenth. This points to a relationship that I find between certain aesthetic theories—particularly those of Kant and Hegel—and the presumptions and practices of later radical art. In subsequent chapters, concepts and works are closer, not only chronologically but in the sense that the "meaning" of the former and the ontological "identity" of the latter are seen to be dependent on the nature of their interaction. Because I attempt to bring artworks and concepts together in a consequential way, I also dwell on intersections between concepts: those processes of grouping that provide contextual grounds for each concept's definition and conditions of use. I call those processes *linkage*. My analysis of linkage identifies a given artistic style with a specific group of concepts, and pairs central works from that style with particular concepts within that group. Although I include such standard aesthetic concepts as form and expression in the discussion, my analysis is not reductive in that it does not posit a "basic" conceptual term from which all other terms can be generated. Basic—or "dominant"—terms are indeed identified, but the emphasis is on their transformations. I hold that a change in concept signals a shift in historical context and, thus, the emergence of new artistic concerns. Accordingly, I take the dominance of a given conceptual term within a group to be a historical event, an indication of an "ascendant" style. The subordinate terms linked to that dominant concept, in effect, bear witness to both the past and the future of that style, to its actual forebears and possible offspring, and thus to shifts in dominance in both terms and works. In chapter 6, I engage in a somewhat technical analysis of this issue.

The notion of conceptual dominance suggests that the concepts I group together are polemical, not merely descriptive. Indeed, I believe that concepts in art importantly function in two ways: as normative and ontic justi-

3

fications. Thus, some concepts ascribe value to historical styles and provide reasons why the art at issue should be seen as ascendant and consequential; others provide reasons why some things or events are properly to be taken as "artworks." However, I do not believe that either concept-type applies independently of the other, and I argue against the notion that something can be taken as an artwork without an assessment of its value. Art that is both modern and radical seems particularly in need of a conceptual "aspect" because its generally antiinstitutional stance precludes the reliance on societal support for ascriptions of artistic status or value. Of course, such estrangement is not uniform: Each radical style has its own institutions to oppose. While the "Academy" may remain a common enemy, other institutional villains range from "decadent social orders" to ideologies that too strictly delimit what an artwork "may or may not be." In chapters 1 and 2, for example, I trace changing villainies by linking "form" with the diverging concepts of "progress" and "expression," and I use this as a way of differentiating between the European and American versions of the avant-garde. In chapter 3 I link the musical avant-garde with the critical concept of social ideals; and in chapters 4 and 5 I take up some artistic assaults on the "limits of appreciation" and on the ontic "durability" of artworks.

My construal of artworks through such terms as "conceptual grouping" and "style" imparts something of a categorical flavor to my discussion. In one sense this is desirable, for it mirrors the proliferation of categories— "positions" and "manifestos"—that typifies the avant-garde. But this is not to say that these activities are to be understood as "consensual" in either origin or projection. Artworks—particularly those self-proclaimed as radical—resist collectivity, and their inclusion within a style generates their competing moves to dominate that style. Thus, the grouping of concepts that I call "linkage" entails a struggle that correlates dominant works with those concepts that most fully account for them. I do not give either works or concepts causal priority over the other. To be sure, the historical emergence of a style entails a conceptual sorting of many works; but, as well, the creation of an individual work entails finding a way of thinking about such creating. Actually, as the very notion of "style" is somewhat artificial, the presumption that styles are coherent as separate entities must be balanced by seeing a coherence in their transformations. This latter view destabilizes style by emphasizing the multiple strains of stylistic origin, by correlating each strain with a competing concept that presumes uniquely to account for that style, and by identifying the artworks that are championed by each such concept. These polemics tend to fade as styles become historically distant, but in the context of recent art the vividness of conceptual conflicts overshadows our sense of the underlying agreements. Actually, I view the apparent stability of historical styles with some suspicion. A stylistic unification of works may signify not coherence but, rather, a capitulation of appreciation to piety—a desire for order that masks the uniqueness of works. It is not the creation of categories that is at issue here, it is their "reification": imputing to style an ontological strength greater than that accorded the individual work. In my discussion of the avant-garde, I emphasize the fragility of this category, and I ascribe this fragility to the recalcitrance of its works in sharing common identities and the reluctance of its concepts in remaining within the bounds of the aesthetic. There are many reasons, for example, why works may not "want to be" as they, variously, are "known to be." Some such reasons are, of course, aesthetic: a needed recasting of relevant qualities. Other reasons, however, may involve intruding obligations of a social or moral type. A recurring theme in my discussion is the interaction of aesthetic and non-aesthetic factors in our accounts of the status and value of artworks.

I devote the first two chapters of this work to the visual arts and develop the concept of the avant-garde through an analysis of two phases: European, c. 1900–38, and American, c. 1945–60. The concept I primarily ascribe to the European phase is "artistic progress" which I locate in the aesthetics of Hegel. I develop this concept through a linkage with such other concepts as abstract and nonobjective art, social and spiritual ideals. In the discussion I show, on the one hand, how the formal achievements of a radical abstract art are justified through the claim that they exemplify an achievable rationality in the social order and, on the other hand, how nonobjective art is linked with the alternative value of "personal transcendence." The artists whose work I emphasize here are Piet Mondrian and Wassily Kandinsky. My discussion of the American avant-garde, in contrast, begins by tracing the concept of form from its roots in the Kantian aesthetics of beauty through its successive linkages with other concepts: genius, creativity, and self-expression. I argue that an ambiguity in the concept of "self" generates an aesthetic polarity in which works strive for transcendence through extreme positions: the purity of "act" or the finality of "stasis." The artists I refer to in this context are Jackson Pollock and Ad Reinhardt.

In chapter 3 I move to a discussion of music, specifically music based upon the "twelve-tone row." Here, my conceptual source is an early theoretical work by Theodor Adorno and his linkage there of radical form in music with social criticism. The composers in question are those Adorno is preoccupied with—Arnold Schoenberg, Alban Berg, Anton Webern—but the issue I focus on goes beyond his concerns. My question is how "criticism" can be said to occur within a musical form so uncompromisingly aloof from both traditional and modern devices of musical "ingratiation." I locate this critical function in the tension between music as a performed, "audible" entity and as a formal, "syntactic" entity. I trace the tension between these to the fact that the formulation of a twelve-tone row and the deployment of that row within a musical work do not depend on whether the "correctness" of such deployment—even in principle—can be heard. I argue that the authenticity of a row's occurrences within a work is a conceptual rather than a perceptual value. Incorporating awareness of that value into appreciation constitutes, by extension, a criticism of the social context in which such awareness—and such values—are absent. This issue develops, through a discussion of musical "fragmentation," into a question about the possibility—or point—of a continuing art under circumstances of formal and social alienation.

In chapter 4 I pursue this inquiry into a more contemporary context in which the distinction that establishes the boundaries between art and non-art becomes the "subject" of the artworks in question. What these works are "about" is the fragility of this distinction, and by obscuring it they come to question the viability of the categories themselves. I raise the question as to whether this categorical "breakdown" generates a novel—and problematical—linkage between aesthetics and ethics. The key concepts here are appreciation and obligation, and they come together in asking whether there are things that "ought not" to be appreciated because of their "centrality" for ethical concerns. The question that follows is whether some such "unappreciables" can, nevertheless, be taken as artworks and, if so, upon what grounds this "inversion" of aesthetic and ethical values can be defended. The "limits of art," here, becomes an issue within—rather than across—historical contexts.

In chapter 5 I reframe this discussion of limits into one about ends, specifically, about whether and how the status of artwork may be lost. Here, I build on Joseph Margolis's concept of "embodiment" and offer a distinction between work and object such that they need not coincide in either their "beginnings" or their "ends." I theorize that artworks enjoy certain (aesthetic) rights and that such rights may conflict with other (nonaesthetic) rights that pertain to entities that are nonworks. These conflicts, in various ways, affect both the ontological status of the work and its duration. One consequence of my argument is the affirmation of such entities as artworks that "endure beyond" their objects, objects that "outlive" their works, and completed works that become "unfinished"—and thereby "end." I suggest that these seemingly counterintuitive proposals are actually quite precise in accounting for the volatility of status in much recent art.

In the last chapter I continue my discussion of the ontology of artworks with particular reference to the theories of George Dickie and Arthur Danto. From this account, I develop a theory of my own. Danto and Dickie both argue that the status of artwork is contextual; for the former it arises within a broad context of conventions—an "artworld"—and for the latter through the attributive actions of "agents" acting in behalf of that world. In order to show the general outlines of this view, I compare it briefly with another, which I call the *exhibited-qualities* view. I contrast them through the correlation each makes between the characteristics that artworks are "known by" and the manner in which something "becomes" art: If the achievement of art status is thought to depend upon the perception of qualities we antecedently know to be "artistic," then the possession of such qualities, for any given thing, is a sufficient condition for this status. I take this to be the exhibited-qualities thesis. On the other hand, if the qualities a thing shows forth come to be known as artistic only as a consequence of an independent attainment of art status, then having such qualities is not constitutive for but merely descriptive of this status. I identify this as the *contextualist* thesis— to which I essentially subscribe. Although this thesis may have broad historical applicability, I limit its demonstration in this book to the avant-garde, for the novel "self-presentations" of this art most easily exemplify what I have to say.

One danger for a thesis that discounts exhibited qualities as a condition for conferring art status is that, without the differentia provided by such qualities, attributive acts can be seen as trivial. I safeguard against this in my own attributive theory by insisting that determinations of artistic status and artistic value are not separable in practice and must cogently be brought together within theory. Here, I part company with Dickie's belief in the separateness of "classificatory" and "evaluative" senses of art, and I analyze his thesis critically and in some detail. I then offer an alternative theory that correlates artistic value and status upon a historical matrix and joins the concept of "candidate for status" with a projection of consequentiality as regards "antecedent" and "future" works. This theory is an account of how artworks achieve status through their claim to some determinate value. This is a claim made to other artworks, some of which are historical, others merely potential. Through this claim, the candidate work seeks acceptance as art from a class of such works in return for the "assurance" that the expanded class of works, when it includes the candidate, will gain in coherence—and value—as a style. This is actually an account of the transformations of artworks in historical time, and, in this sense, chapter 6 functions as a formal exposition of the aesthetic position merely outlined in the earlier chapters. It also functions as a summation of previous material by giving examples of how an artwork introduced within alternative contexts—as a member of differing "tradition classes"—can be interpreted through the general theory.

My basic approach in this book goes against some recent currents in that I do not side with either works or their interpretations. I do not believe, for example, that art is self-referential and best discussed by pointing out the "good-(or bad-)making features" that influence its enjoyment. On the other hand, I do not believe that what artworks come to is "just" the ongoing series of their (interesting) interpretations. This latter view, I admit, is more seductive than the former for it keeps us apprehensive whereas the other smacks too much of leisure and "collectibles." Nevertheless, I reject both these views for I believe that while art can be—or be about—anything at all, it never is. But what this "is" comes to is not decidable, even in principle, either through a cataloguing of "features" or through the accumulation of "interpretations."

One problem with the foregoing remarks is that they can be interpreted as a brief for relativism, to be supported by the observation that as time passes we accommodate both interpretations and their subjects to our changing needs. Although such a notion may in fact be true, it is, however, trivially so, for it tells us nothing about the content of our choices—only that they probably change. Such relativism, like an underdeveloped country, survives on imports. The imports here are the (nonrelativist) grounds for identifying relevant works and ascriptions of value. So I must resist this charge by commenting briefly on the grounds underlying my own choice of imports. This is really a question of "metainterpretation," which, as such, is not my central concern, but some self-reflection here may help the reader across the larger transitions between the chapters that follow.

I suspect that the nature of art is like that of the perfectly moral act: fleeting, elusive, much sought after, yet seldom experienced or even recognized. In this sense the antagonist of art is its institutionalization—whether social or theoretical. Institutionalizing art is much like placing Pharaoh inside the pyramid: The fact of death is denied, and the stirrings of spirit are hidden from view. One thing that seems to distinguish modern art from art of other periods—prior and subsequent—is its pattern of reactions against institutions. It is not just the "bohemianism"—the familiar "skewering of the bourgeoisie"—that shows this; more importantly, it is the reaction of artworks against their historically assigned "passivity." One mark of this reaction is the conviction that artworks must assume—indeed, appropriate—responsibility for their "meanings" and that they do this by including "what they are about" in their ontologies. This thesis of reciprocal aboutness, in which works and theories are seen as "accounting for each other," is mirrored in my title, *Art and Concept*, and I see it as identifying a major characteristic of the avant-garde. In developing this thesis, I often speak of works and concepts in such volitional terms—as if they were the authors of their own uses. However, I do not mean these locutions to be hypostases of unlikely metaphysical entities; I offer them simply as devices through which I avoid the often tedious circumlocution to actions of human agents.

The targets that artworks identify in their "reaction against passivity" are those institutional practices that deny reciprocity to work and concept by attempting to delimit the subject of discourse—to fix the "boundaries of art." Such delimitations act to separate, for example, beauty from morality, objects from actions, status from value, art from nonart, frameworks into their insides and outsides. Each of my chapters is concerned with an artistic attempt to put aside one or more such delimitations which, in the historical circumstances, had come to be perceived as repressive rather than merely descriptive. But, together with these reactions, in the climate of protest risks also occur—of a kind that traditional allegiances, however repressive, protect against. There are risks, for example, of fragmentation, anomie, indifference, despair, cooptation, and I discuss these by aligning them with the artistic ambitions that give them rise.

Finally, there is this consideration: Modern art has often been characterized as an activity that is essentially "about itself" and, in this sense, is largely free of the didactic and moral preoccupations of older art. Such practices as abstraction in the visual arts, atonality in music, syntactic invention in literature have all been adduced in support of this interpretation. My view is quite different, for I take such an interpretation to misconceive the semantic nature of the new art by insisting that its theoretic component is irrelevant to its proper appreciation. I offer the contrary thesis—as outlined above—that what a work "says" or "shows" includes what is said or shown about it, for I include the theoretic component of a work in its identity as art. Seen from this view, avant-garde art is profoundly moral and didactic—but not self-evidently so. It is, after all, a "radical" art, and the "difficulty" of appreciation—the new demands on the audience—is also part of its content. The historical dilution and eventual withdrawal of such demands may, indeed, have signified the close of this period and the emergence of the art and concerns of our present day. That transformation is another story, however, but one for which this study would hope to have some value.

ONE

Hegel, "Progress," and the Avant-Garde in Europe

This chapter discusses the European phase of the avant-garde, its theoretical debt to the philosophy of Hegel, and some consequences of its scrupulous attention to this debt. The focus here is on the visual arts, primarily on painting, during the years in which such theory and practice first developed and flourished: c. 1900–45. To help identify the area of discussion, I distinguish between the art-historical categories *modern* and *avant-garde* and consider the latter a subset of the former. I interpret "modern art" as a loose consensus term that refers to a large body of works after—roughly—1860 whose stylistic affinities are sufficiently strong to distinguish them as a whole from works based on older traditions. I use the term "avant-garde" to name a small group of modern works that show specific reliance on such Hegelian concepts as progress and transcendence. I construe such works to be "theory-laden," not only because much has been written about them but because some of what was written—often by the artists themselves—purports to justify the works in relation to broad historical trends.[1] Both theories and works take the polemical form of identifying—and personifying—advanced stages in the "inevitable" course of such trends.

I do not, however, view the avant-garde as a monolithic phenomenon. Rather, I distinguish two theoretical components, *abstraction* and *nonobjectivity*, and I differentiate them through their emphases, respectively, on the formal or experiential interpretation of the concept of progress. My major protagonists in this discussion are the painters Piet Mondrian and Wassily Kandinsky, both of whom enjoy dominant positions in the avant-garde. Each of these positions exhibits a remarkable congruity between artwork and theoretical writing, and their comparison, I submit, supports the distinction I am attempting here.

II

Much of avant-garde theory is self-consciously historical.[2] Works are understood as exemplars of particular historical trends and developments and are judged for their adequacy in this role as well as for their "internal" aesthetic qualities. Such theory, evidently, has strong Hegelian roots. Art itself, for Hegel, is but an episode in historical time. Within the Hegelian world view—the "evolution of spirit in time"—art is limited in its role as an exemplar of historical development. The effectiveness of art as a symbol of culture is relegated only to those periods in history where the sensuous components of artworks have not yet become a hindrance to the progressive "self-consciousness" of spirit.[3]

The antagonism that energizes the Hegelian dialectic is between "matter" and "spirit," the inertia of the concrete present inhibiting the larger freedom of new possibilities. But the triadic scheme of the dialectic converts simple opposition into a process whereby possibility is made actual only to be transcended by further possibility. For Hegel, the "ideal" is not a Kantian "regulatory principle" but, rather, is conceived as an occurrence in actual time.[4]

In one sense, the Hegelian ideal is the conclusion of all historical process, such conclusion defined as not only the end of a most comprehensive sequence but the teleological "reason" or "goal" of that sequence. In another—also Hegelian—sense, this ideal has numerous occurrences, each marking a "victory of spirit," one episode in time when a particular development achieves its maximal expression and must be redefined anew. The development I am concerned with here is the history of art under an interpretation of its "completion" and subsequent redefinition. Of course, if the history of art is simply a chronology of the production of artworks, the thesis of its completion is an evident absurdity; to the present day the activity continues and expands. But Hegel construes history in a way that is illuminating on this issue: "History" in his formulation is located within but is not synonymous with the development of culture. It is, rather, only a discrete part, one that completes itself at the juncture where an ideal of freedom and the fact of human autonomy come together. That achievement of spirit where "freedom" gains ascendancy in individual affairs marks the end of history—although not of culture.[5] The distinction wanted here can be indicated by the observation that freedom attained can be perfected but not transcended. In Marxist political theory, the proletarian revolution is the instrumentality for achieving this stage. In certain aesthetic theories—those I call avant-garde—particular types of abstract and nonobjective art are also offered as culminations of the history of art.

For Hegel, artworks are considered as revelatory symbols of the stages of cultural development. But, as with history proper, the history of art includes the "end" of art, and the evolution of art forms shows "progress" toward this end. Formal change and incrementation of value proceed together here. Progress, when predicated of art history, implies that late art is "better" in some important way than is early art. To be effective, this thesis must be ruthless toward "deviant" or "retrogressive" works. Not all recent works, for example, are better—only those that "truly" reveal their time.[6] However, if the "best" art is also that which threatens to conclude its own tradition, then it must show the signs of that tradition's approaching obsolescence. In Hegel's complex theory of value, a distinction is made between art as it measures *culture* and art as *it* is measured within its own tradition. This is a distinction between what is the *best* art and what is *most completely* art. The latter criterion requires a notion of the ideal constituents of artworks qua art. This notion returns us to the historical tension between matter and spirit. Although culture is "well rid" of its material encumbrances at each point in its development, art remains, at every such point, a sensuous symbol. This suggests that the "most complete" form of art has a certain equilibrium between matter and spirit—between *what* is symbolized and the symbol's sensuous embodiment.[7]

Thus, progress in art is seen as in conflict with "perfection" in art, and the ensuing dialectic leads inferentially to the "end" of art. The value of late art rests in what it presents, but this value is a function of historical position, of what—at different times—*can* be presented. The "incompleteness" of late art is found in its striving to remain a viable symbol despite the historical ascendancy of verbal over auditory and plastic form. Hegel, as we know, stacks his three stages of artistic evolution—symbolic, classic, and romantic—and identifies poetry as the highest form of the late (romantic) stage. However, discourse is the medium of cognitive thought as well as poetry. The "highest" form of art, then, has the potential for further change by coming to resemble what is not art, namely, philosophy.[8]

But the Hegelian price for this development in "late" art is that art relinquish a constitutive element of its identity, namely, its sensuousness. This historical quandary suggests two alternatives, each with its own risk: (a) Art takes refuge in past traditions and risks trivialization through the loss of symbolic efficacy, that is, the risk that art-making becomes a conventionalized activity and artworks no longer function as symbols of "progress in culture"; (*b*) specific art forms strive to transcend, variously, the limitations of their sensate characteristics and risk their separate identities, that is, the risk that, if the subclasses constituting the class of all and only artworks no longer differentiate among themselves, then the extended class may well fail to constitute a unique symbol type. Blurring such distinctions as hold between painting and music may, in effect, threaten the boundary between art and non-art.

III

It is evident in Hegel's remarks on the particular arts that he did not envision the developments we now call modern art. Certainly, the examples he chose for his three "romantic" subcategories give little evidence that he was concerned with the currents of art-making in his own time.[9] Evidently, then, the quandary I speak of above is not one that Hegel proposes, but I do believe it to be part of his legacy. The lofty role that Hegel assigns to art—as a symbol of "spiritual transcendence"—provides later radical movements with a reason for their ambitions, even if they must look elsewhere for their procedures. The alternative (*b*) listed above—the risk of symbolic uniqueness—was the alternative of choice for the avant-garde, as it was perceived to contain the possibility of a new category of art from which the aesthetics of naturalistic beauty and mimetic "service" are excluded. The threat to the identity of art through loss of its discriminability is faced up to by positing a new content for discrimination. This replacement of content constitutes a shift from the *representation* of cultural ideals to the *presentation* of cultural criticism. A recurring theme in fin-de-siècle social criticism is the repressive and stagnant nature of its own society.[10] At this historical juncture, the imperative for art is to retain its own vitality. Within avant-garde theory, it attempts this by assuming the mantle of historical progress *for itself* and by acting, through the nature of its own development, as a *rebuke* to the society at large. In a "decadent" society, one that thwarts its own potential for progress, aesthetic symbols that are ordinarily affirmative need become negative in order to reveal the social malaise. Criticism cannot, however, be projected through conventional, "popular," means, for this only serves to reinforce decadence in that the "matter" of criticism is couched in forms that, paradoxically, suggest approval of the status quo. The critical content of radical art, to the contrary, is transmitted through its formal estrangement. The orthodox Hegelian notion of art as cultural exemplification assumes that *what* is exemplified is ascendant rather than degenerate in a culture. "Decadence" can be understood here as a culture's willful rejection of an *under-stood* possibility of its own progress. The force of avant-garde aesthetics lies in its move to usurp the forms of progress from the culture proper and locate them in works of art. Radical art functions as criticism because it exemplifies what its society *should* evolve into but has not. Such art, then, serves both as a reproach and as a concrete instance of progress. It seeks the ontological status of the very reality it symbolizes.[11] It is this "hubris" that differentiates avant-garde art from its predecessors.

Hegel's own political conservatism, his need to reconcile progress with the power of the state, did not permit him the notion of a counterculture avant-garde. For him, progress or "evolution of spirit" is manifest both in institutions of culture and in the circumstances of individual life.[12] Because of his aversion to dualities, Hegel sees no ultimate conflict between the needs of the state and those of persons. Yet, as has been amply evident, the balance is seldom maintained. From the standpoint of the state, its relations with individuals—its citizens—are centered in the statistical measure of the support it is given—or can command. From the standpoint of the individual, accord between the collective program and personal fulfillment is a happenstance, something to be hoped for but a test of conscience when it does not occur. The criteria for success in each case are also different. Progress is properly a function of a collective, and it is measured through "objective" symbols of "revision" and "expansion." For the individual, progress is more aptly called "transcendence," and it is measured through "subjective" symbols of "awareness" and "fulfillment." To describe such distinctions as tensions suggests that the formal aesthetic criteria satisfying a cultural telos may run counter to the expressive needs of a particular community or individual artist. This marks a tension between a culture's quest for symbols that satisfy its projections of renewal and an individual's quest for symbols of existential meaning.

From a conservative standpoint, of course, neither of these quests need be undertaken: Rejecting the demands of a cultural telos can be interpreted as a return to past forms in order to cope with, or escape, present dilemmas. Ignoring the uniqueness of individual experience, on the other hand, is a way of avoiding the isolation and anxiety of personal identity through an identification with collective norms. Within a radical framework, however, we find little sympathy for the traditionalism or eclecticism that identifies with other points of view. This is particularly true of the avant-garde movements within modern art. Yet, even here, the tension between collective and individual values persists. As my thesis is that both the concept of artistic progress and its differing manifestations have a common Hegelian source,

I continue my discussion by examining the multiple criteria of aesthetic value that can be found within Hegel's "division of the arts."

IV

When the possibilities of art-making are interpreted through a scheme of formal rules, this inevitably imposes a limitation on individual artistic choice. Such a restriction can be interpreted as a Platonic echo of the subordination of aesthetic impulses to a higher wisdom. Hegel, unlike Plato in this regard, considers the most complete expression of human freedom to be—at the same time—the most perfect expression of historical "inevitability."[13] This accord is, of course, theological in origin: a premise of cumulative harmony between the exercise of human will and the "divine plan." For the individual artist, such a harmony entails the confluence of what is possible with what is permissible. This is a situation in which no considered alternative can endanger the program through which the movement holding the artist's allegiance is defined. If this harmony fails or—as is more likely—is never totally achieved, the choice remains as to how progress is measured: through the "authenticity" of a symbol's formal qualities or through its power as a "testimonial" of experience.

Hegel's strategy for overcoming a conflict is to subject it to dialectical scrutiny. Here, I take this only to mean placing alternative positions onto a temporal scale of value and, thus, showing them each to be incomplete yet sequential expressions of a historical logos. The forms of art constitute a particular type of temporal succession and are thus one expression of "progress in culture." Yet, as I discuss above, such progress is variously interpreted, and the value its forms are assigned is bound up with the criteria through which artworks are assessed. Hegel's criteria of aesthetic value are not systematically developed, but his categorization of art forms does suggest certain alternative standpoints from which the "particular arts" are to be viewed and ranked.[14] I identify four such standpoints and discuss them in turn:

1. *The place of an art within the total span of cultural history.* Here, the value is placed on the art form that surpasses all others through its capacity to exemplify the highest development of "idea" thus far achieved within historical time. This value is limited only by the limitations inherent in the sensuous nature of aesthetic symbols. As art is a part of but is not coextensive with culture, certain cultural ideals eventually evolve beyond the possibility of sensuous presentation and can only be couched in the more spiritually "potent" symbols of religion or, ultimately, philosophy. Hegel's chosen art

form for this category is poetry, the "highest" form of romantic art. Because poetry is discursive and of all the arts is thus closest to philosophy, the poetic work encompasses the highest conceptual value of which art is capable. But from another standpoint (4) poetry is flawed as art because its medium—discourse—lacks the concrete sensuous immediacy of a form—classical sculpture—in which concept and sensuousness are in "perfect balance."

2. *The place of an art within the history of an individual culture.* Here, an art form is valued for its capacity to exemplify its own culture, however small the achievement of that culture—in the total historical span—may actually be. Hegel identifies architecture, for example, as a symbolic art and thus as the prime exemplar of a time and place, the ancient East, when "spirit" is only dimly perceived and inchoately expressed. Yet, what can then *be* expressed is best expressed in architecture because, unlike the other arts, architecture is stylistically congruent, through its "overdependency" on matter, with the conceptual limitations of that culture. Hegel sees, for example, the Egyptian pyramid, in its heaviness and inertia, as offering a place to the physical god whose spirit, because it is prematurely evoked, does not enter.

3. *An art as measured by the changes in dominance, transculturally, among the arts.* Here, the various arts gain or lose value as they move toward or away from the historical period they best exemplify. Architecture, for example, may be the prime exemplar of symbolic art, but it gives way to sculpture in the classic period. Paradoxically, classical architecture may be more "spiritual" than its symbolic counterpart and thus, from the standpoint of criterion 1, of greater value. From the standpoint of criterion 4, the sculpted Greek figure, in its presentation of divinity through an idealized human image is, for Hegel, the highest classical art form. But under criterion 3, sculpture, in its turn, shows its own limitations and gives way to painting, the earliest of the romantic forms. There is a certain valuational "pathos" to be found in this construal of art forms that gain early ascendancy in Hegel's historical progression only to be later "transcended." For a given art form, once its role as cultural exemplar is over, any further aesthetic development is seen to be "parasitic" on the characteristics of the then "dominant" form. The pathos arises out of the purported inevitability of this process, an inevitability which, as I shall show, is itself brought into question in avant-garde art.

4. *An art as measured by the balance between its "spiritual" and "sensuous" components.* For Hegel, progress in culture constitutes a progressive triumph of the "idea" over its material vehicle, a "disembodiment" of spirit. Art in its role as cultural exemplar shows this, too, and thus the inference

arises, as in standpoints 1 and 3, that art increases in value throughout historical time. This "contest" takes place both within and between individual art forms as they strive for historical adequacy. In the latter case we find, as in romantic art, that painting's illusionistic accomplishments are superseded by the notational and temporal freedom of music which, in turn, gives way to poetry's direct appeal to the imagination. However, where Hegel identifies classical sculpture as not only the dominant form of its time but as the "most perfect" art, he establishes still another criterion of value, one by which the later romantic arts are found *lacking*. His standpoint shifts from art-in-culture to art-as-art, for the perfection of sculpture is found in the equivalence of its balance between sensuality and spirit. Indeed, this notion evokes the balance in temperament that Platonic philosophy seeks for virtue in human conduct. The achievement of classical sculpture, under this criterion, is that of an ideal made actual: Although it was realized in history, it is not susceptible to further revision through history. It thus remains a standard that defines the type but is no longer attainable. Within this last criterion we discern a certain nostalgia in Hegel's concept of progress—the inevitability of loss as well as gain.

The influence of Hegel's aesthetic theories on the programs of the avant-garde is quite complex. Not all of his doctrine of historical progress in the arts can be uniformly interpreted as positive. Also to be found are discouraging sentiments, particularly in those instances when Hegel seems to take back what he promises—whenever an emphasis on change threatens to obscure categorical stability. In the division of the arts, for all of his preoccupation with time and transformation, Hegel's categories remain rigid. The arts wax and wane according to the limitations of their formal natures, and there seems no redress—no place for "self-help." In section III, I speak of the hubris of the avant-garde as the move to usurp the content of progress from the larger society for art's own symbolic ends. Rather than succumb to categorical limitations, individual arts strive to supersede *themselves* in order to avoid being superseded by others. The formal and referential "constants" that, heretofore, provided each art with its own categorical identity, become the targets of this effort.[15] Tampering with an identity is risky business, but, at that level of "self-consciousness," failure to do so would be to deny the basic notion of progress in art and sink into an academic traditionalism. In section II I describe the avant-garde's alternative to be that where "specific art forms strive to transcend the limitations of their sensate characteristics." My discussion here of Hegel's value categories purports to show the theoretical source of the concept of limitation although, to be sure, this concept is differently expressed within each category. Indeed, one of the strengths of Hegel's analysis is his rejection of a single uniform basis for aesthetic value in favor of multiple bases which become relevant under varying circumstances and for different questions. I suggest that criterion 3—the historical shifts of dominance between the arts—is the most applicable to avant-garde concerns precisely because it is the most threatening.

If we read Hegel's theory one way, from a holistic standpoint, it seems rigid in the way it imparts a teleological sense of inevitability to process. For individual art practices, this can degenerate into a sense of futility or complacency in that the value of a work is seen as a factor of historical position and not of individual effort. Read another way, under the guise of "freedom," Hegel offers a more flexible basis for historical change which, at any specific time, can be understood as providing both a warning and a guide to creative activity. Hegel's third criterion signals, within his romantic epoch, a clear progression from painting to music to poetry. However, although the distinctions between art forms may have been self-evident in the nineteenth century, they ceased being so in the twentieth. In this latter context, the proper choice of formal characteristics became the means for artistic survival, and, accordingly, those "belonging to" one art became subject to usurpation by another art—all in the name of averting a threatened "historical obsolescence." For the avant-garde, this effort entailed a reconstruction of the "matter-spirit" ratio within an individual art—a "discarding" and/or "purifying" of everything "inert"—based upon the model presented by the art form occupying a "higher" place in the Hegelian hierarchy of value. I pursue this thesis below through an analysis of the art here at issue: painting.

v

The self-transcending activities of the avant-garde in painting did not result in a uniform "radical style." In fact, I distinguish two main developments within this effort, which I label *abstract* and *nonobjective* and which I take to derive from the two interpretations of progress that I identify above as collective and individual. However, I do not take the differences in question to be so fundamental as to cast doubt on the inclusive category: avant-garde.[16] Before I discuss these differences, therefore, some mention of features constitutive of the category is in order. One such supporting feature is that included artworks all exemplify certain changes in pictorial form that developed during the latter part of the nineteenth century.[17] These changes modified earlier illusionistic practices which are based upon concepts of object discreteness and of the separate identities of space and time. In such "traditional" paintings—for our purposes, Western painting between Giotto and Courbet—the use of perspective schemata in representation presumes a holistic, invariant state of affairs in which depicted objects are located in an optically three-dimensional space. If we disregard certain stylistic and icono-graphic variations, we can interpret all such objects as occurring in that given space at the *same time*. The scanning of a perspective schema discloses rules for determining relative size and position in simultaneous occurrences. The viewer, having the security of indefinite access to the *enduring* moment of the picture's time, is free to indulge his *ongoing* time in savoring the various qualities and relationships of the depicted "place."[18] This "frozen moment" of perspectival illusion, which had previously been considered a source of pictorial richness, becomes a target of avant-garde criticism. Some aspects of this criticism sound an orthodox Hegelian note: that the demands of con-sciousness "now" favor process over architectonic. Other aspects rely on the Hegel of later radical sociology: Appreciation, for example, of perspectival illusion, assumes enjoyment of an atavistic leisure, a leisure of actual time that is ill-gotten and exclusive and that is lavishly committed to the ex-perience of a socially conservative illusion of timelessness—or status quo.

An art form that is heedful of this criticism must supplant perspective with a "new" schema that, in some way, embodies the factor of process. The hall-mark of this new schema I identify as *noncumulative scanning*, that is, abolition of any set standard of relative position through which all marks on the picture surface can be interpreted as occurring in a given place at the same time. In the absence of such regulators as vanishing point, horizon line, and so on, acts of scanning do not generate a progressive realization of *one* pictorial structure but, rather, reveal *indefinitely many* structures, each authentically but not uniquely constitutive of the painting. Under this schema, marks on the surface can be equally interpreted as belonging to form or to space, and *no* mark is in constant relation with any other mark, the rela-tionships varying with changes in direction of the viewer's eye movements. Instead of symbolizing a timeless depiction of a single moment, the avant-garde painting thus presents itself as a symbol configurating in real time— the time of the viewer's appreciative process—the individual act of look-ing.[19] Yet, this catholicity in elements and configurations, if not subsumed under some new principles of ordering, could result in an unwanted random-ness.[20] The formal constraints of older art were supported not only by distinctions between objects and space but by the hierarchies of value these objects and their groupings represent, hierarchies that can be taken to mirror the social values of the larger culture. When such constraints were removed others were introduced, although, to be sure, these new constraints were couched in the rhetoric of aesthetic and social "freedom." The distinctions I indicate above, between abstract and nonobjective art, I take to be two construals of pictorial ordering that are central in the historical ascendancy of the avant-garde. I undertake their analysis by relating them to the tension I note in section III between two justifications for the ideal of "historical progress." The pairings come out as follows: collective–abstract and individual–nonobjective. I discuss each in turn.

VI

The term "abstract" is commonly opposed to the term "representational," thereby indicating a distinction between mimetic and nonmimetic styles. But "abstract" is also used in the sense that "all art is abstract." This usage can be taken to mean that the "essential" activity common to all pictorial style is that of abstracting, that is, the selection of just those visual phenomena deemed most significant for particular stylistic purposes. Therefore, the claim that one method or style of painting is more "realistic" than another reduces to a difference in attitudes about the fit of certain perceptual qualities for a given *convention* of representation.[21] In this usage, the central notion is that differences in style are not differences in fidelity to perceptual subjects, only differences in the arrays of qualities considered. Here, the distinction between "representation" and "abstraction" is a distinction between the generality and particularity of the qualities transcribed.

When this notion of generality is joined with a self-conscious historicism, however, a sense of "abstract" emerges that identifies the theory with which I am concerned. Here the claim is that the degree of generality *increases* over the course of European art history and that this increase becomes the *subject* of art in its late (advanced) stages.[22] The term "generality" here becomes synonymous with "universality" and its association of "underlying," "essential," "basic," and so on. This is where the concept of abstraction becomes polemical and establishes its affinity with the Hegelian notion of progress in history. The artist, for example, is given the (historical) *obligation* to reveal the underlying constants in pictorial experience, to distinguish between the essential and the transitory, and to discard, to the degree possible, all pictorial material that would obscure this distinction. "To the degree possible" identifies another Hegelian tenet, namely, that progress is achieved through "work."[23] Forms must be created and then tested to see if they fit their role as universals at that cognized moment in history. The inevitable false starts are to be overcome by a *collective* commonality of purpose among artists. This emphasis on the "collective" gives the artistic enterprise a quasi-scientific character—that of "research" into nature's or, better, spirit's unfolding mysteries. Within this theory of abstraction, the term "abstraction" moves from identification of process, that is, *abstracting from* nature, to identification of a state of being, namely, art that *is abstract.* This second usage marks a historical moment when a procedural self-consciousness is joined with authenticated universals through the purification of formal means. The result is so "complete" yet "unadorned" that, in a certain sense, it cannot be improved upon: The search for essential form is not construed as one indefinitely open to culture-bound reinterpretations; it ends when the forms underlying natural appearances are isolated and authenticated.

One characteristic of this construal of "abstraction" is that it generates a goal-oriented process: the search for formal bases or essences. If one accepts the Hegelian premise that such goals are not merely regulatory but are achievable in actual historical time, the question arises as to how one accounts for further change once such a goal is achieved. If abstract art, for example, "completes" the historical process of abstraction, how and why would abstract works continue to be produced? One answer to this question might be that continuing change could be sustained through an expansion of art into the nonaesthetic. This would constitute a version of the cultural criticism discussed in section III. One justification of this expansion into the nonaesthetic would be in the transfer of "virtues" achieved by abstract art into the workings of its larger society. The argument, here, might go as follows: If the search for essences in natural appearance is both cogent and successful, then these essences, once found, might be presumed to have a value that is not limited to their function in works of art. Inasmuch as this search also includes our living environment as its subject, might not this environment, then, be bettered—purified of antique clutter—by a methodical application of essentialist principles? Thus, artwork, artifact, building, the organization of communities, even ethical precepts, are all potential for such purification. In this way, a "pan-aestheticism" replaces the older theory of autonomous art and presumes to function less as a propaedeutic to better art than to a more rational life. The criterion of aesthetic uniqueness here becomes devalued, and an artwork is seen to function as a sample that guides the proper development of other social structures through the information it provides.[24] Presumably, as any of a number of "properly formed" abstractions are each adequate bearers of information, their aesthetic ranking relative to each other becomes secondary to their utility for visual-social undertakings.

The Dutch artist Piet Mondrian based his work upon a carefully formu-

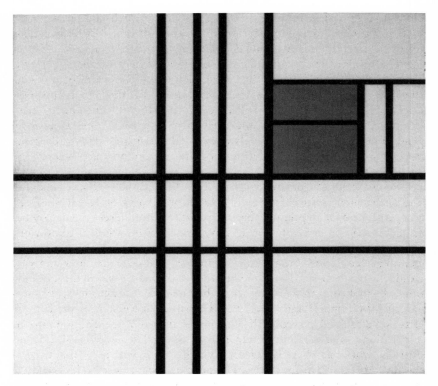

Piet Mondrian, *Composition, 1936* (1936). Oil on canvas, 28¾ × 26".
Philadelphia Museum of Art: The Louise and Walter Arensberg Collection.
Photographed by Philadelphia Museum of Art.

lated set of essentialist "neoplastic" principles. Their progressive realization
in the paintings he made between 1900 and 1944 provides us with perhaps
the most austere and consistent example of the process of abstraction in
avant-garde art. His choice of a rectilinear format rests upon the thesis that
axes and vectors instantiated by diagonals, curves, and so on, must find their
"resolutions" in the vertical-horizontal. Similarly, his reduction of color to
the primary colors plus black and white is justified by the thesis that the
makeup of all other parts of the spectrum is composite—thus "fugitive"—
and must be resolved into the primaries. His use of form is governed by scale,
position, and color but *not* by uniqueness of character or reference. Through

this destruction of "particularity," Mondrian purports to overcome the classical distinction between form and space and to rid his paintings of any vestige of literary narrative. In his later works, Mondrian moved away from the classicism of his middle period to a direct concern for pictorial rhythm achieved through the fragmentation of form. The titles of these paintings have an evocative reference to jazz music: *Broadway Boogie-Woogie, Victory Boogie-Woogie*. This approximation of a musical ideal strikes a distinctly Hegelian note, for music is here viewed as free from certain limitations that persist even within "advanced" nonmimetic pictorial art. These limitations are located in the association of plastic form with weight and place. Thus, Mondrian's search for a "pure plastic" equivalent of musical rhythm is a way of overcoming such pictorial "materiality"—an instance of the self-consciousness of the avant-garde I refer to above.[25] I return to this theme in my discussion of nonobjective art.

Mondrian did not consider his paintings and their guiding principles merely to be articulations of a personal expression or style. Rather, he saw them as neutral and "objective" and hence as available—indeed, "recommended"—to all practitioners in the visual arts. He was one of the first of avant-garde artists to speculate about the obsolescence of easel painting and, in this sense, he adduced a Hegelian linkage between artistic autonomy and the end of art. The *casualty* within his theory is the value of "personal expression," one that usually is positively associated with the avant-garde. Although this notion of self-expression may be historically understood as the egalitarian offspring of the older, more elitist, notion of genius, it remains a mandate for the artist to follow his private vision and forge an individual style. For the utopian ambitions of Mondrian, however, this "subjectivity" works against the "objective historical fact" of the discovery and articulation of artistic universals. Personal expression, then, unless at the service of these universals, is viewed as decadent or arbitrary. The main objective, here, is the achievement of a purely nonrepresentational art, and Mondrian sees this achievement as a turning point in the history of art—as the ascendancy of "the culture of determined relations" over the "culture of particular forms." From this point there is no return, and the "compromises" with representational imagery as found in surrealism, or with "partial" abstraction as found in cubism, are, for Mondrian, merely delays in the inevitable dominance of abstract art. He sees the artist's participation in this process as requiring an acquiescence to its impersonal demands. This is achieved through a freedom *from* subjectivity, "from individual sentiments," and "from the domination of the individual inclination within him."[26] The familiar struggle indicated here—of reason against inclination—equates individual freedom with the affirmation of specific (rational) choice but not with free enactment of choice. The artist, for example, who makes the wrong choice—who paints an ideologically unsupportable painting—is not historically or objectively free although he may have the experience or illusion of freedom. The teleological Hegel is here very much in evidence.

VII

Nonobjective art shares a historicist basis with abstraction, but the process of development is described very differently. Although nonobjectivity is also a creature of the "evolution of spirit," its occurrence does not mark a point on a continuum; rather, it is seen as discontinuous with the past, a unique event, an invention of spirit essentially free of the formal and referential preoccupations of past art. A nonobjective work is not a distillation of essences from the manifold of natural appearances; rather, it is part of a new specification of pictorial meaning which it shares with other nonobjective works.

We note that the term "nonobjective" occurs as a negation and thus presumably excludes the realm of objects from its reference. This exclusion can be interpreted in a number of ways: First, nonobjective forms, as noted above, do not represent forms of appearance, and neither are they to be considered distillates or abstractions of such forms. They are, rather, independent inventions that refer to (a different aspect of) the world through a program of positive affinities that replaces the mimetic reference. This program shifts the referential relationship from works and objects to works and *feelings*. The reference type, unlike the case of visual resemblance, does not occur between symbolic entities within the same sense realm. Here, the correlation occurs between a visual symbol and a referent—feelings—that does not constitute a sense realm at all. Music is the art form typically identified with a direct expression or evocation of feelings. The term "direct" indicates the absence of mediation through depictive or descriptive properties. The much argued question about how or whether this is possible does not concern me here. What is at issue is why, at a certain point, visual artists took this symbol-type to be one worthy of emulation. In section VI, I note Mondrian's interest in the formal properties of musical rhythm; but he has little to say about emotive "equivalents." Before I discuss counterpart theories in nonobjective art, some comments on the general relation of this issue to Hegelian theory are needed.

In a progress-centered aesthetic, there is the concern, as I indicate in section II, with purifying the artwork of all "material excess." Particular forms of art can then presumably be graded for their success in furthering the ideal of dematerialization. If such a hierarchy of value can be constructed *within* an art form, that is, as a comparison of styles, it also seems plausible to construct one *between* forms. In Hegel's thesis of the historical "succession" of art forms, within the category of romantic art, painting is superseded as the dominant art form by music. Hegel had reasons for this: The fact that music is an art of duration rather than extension identifies it as an art of process rather than of place. It is therefore "closer" than painting to the temporal flows of both history and emotional experience. Music is also patently nonrepresentational, and it avoids reference to the concrete entities of the material world. For visual art to take music as a paradigm of success, therefore, requires a program through which musical "virtues" can be emulated. The problem that painting faces in this undertaking is to avoid "capitulating" to music; that is, painting must remain visual—a mute physical object—and yet take on music's perceived advantages for itself.

The artist I propose as the main protagonist of nonobjective theory is Mondrian's contemporary, the Russian painter Wassily Kandinsky. The works I have in mind are those painted after 1919 when Kandinsky abandoned his lyrical-amorphous forms in favor of a geometric approach. Unlike the reductive isomorphism found in Mondrian's paintings, Kandinsky emphasizes differences in *kind* as well as in scale and placement within his geometric lexicon. For Mondrian, as noted in section VI, the basic formal relationship is the right angle—the guarantor of "rationality" that underlies all variation. Kandinsky's work exhibits no such underlying consistency. Rather, forms relate through the "pressure" of their individual differences upon each other. Consequently, within each act of scanning, forms change in impact, position, *and* identity—thereby establishing novel groupings as form-types shift in their family allegiances. What a painting comes to, in this context, is a temporal unity achieved through the sequential experience; it is not—as is a Mondrian—a spatial unity based on the reciprocal "neutralization" of the color-shapes. Kandinsky made frequent use of the musical term "fugue" in his titles. The reference to musical polyphony is not casual for it points to much of the substance of Kandinsky's efforts. This includes the ongoing fluctuation in groupings and dispersals found in his compositions; the unique arrays of invented forms—perhaps the most varied geometric lexicon achieved in that period; the preference for contrapuntal over harmonic structure, for flow over hierarchy, for open-endedness over resolution.[27]

It is noteworthy that Kandinsky did not subscribe to the "historical inevitability" of nonrepresentational art. His Hegelianism is directed at the "liberation of consciousness," and he theorizes that artistic advance shows

Vasily Kandinsky, *Composition 8* (July 1923). Oil on canvas, 55⅛ × 79⅛".
Collection, Solomon R. Guggenheim Museum, New York.
Photographed by Robert E. Mates.

itself through *individual* freedom from categorical restraints. The antagonism between mimetic and nonmimetic form, which is at the basis of the theory of abstraction, is not as significant for nonobjective theory, for there feeling is primary, and its presentation is value-neutral as to the modality of form. This may be shown through the admiration Kandinsky professes for the French "primitive" realist Henri Rousseau who, "[because of the] complete and exclusive simplicity of his representation . . . ring[s] forth the sound of the internal."[28]

This catholicity affirms not only that both representation and nonrepresentation remain historically viable approaches for the avant-garde but that the identification of symbol-type—the referential mode—is a variable dependent upon interpretation. The presumption, for example, that mimetic images can invoke the "internal" is paralleled by the thought that nonmimetic images can invoke the "world of appearances." A case in point is found in the writings of Paul Klee, Kandinsky's Bauhaus associate. Klee, in a combinant verbal and graphic work, invites us on "a little trip into the land of deeper insight." This is, in fact, a journey through a drawing where the graphic evocations identified as "rivers," "woods," "a child with bright curls," interchange with evocations of "joy," "repressed anxiety," "optimism," and so on.[29] I note here that this double reference to objects and feelings occurs through a form-type that—in the ordinary sense—has little mimetic character. Yet it does not follow, for Klee, that the pictorial function of his elements is limitable to their purely formal interaction. These pictorial elements differ from those in abstract works in that they are nonobjective inventions which, because they are not reductions of appearances, can share the *particularistic* character of the world of objects. They function through instantiating the differences—accords and discords—between events that transform a sequence into a journey: an experience of narrative. I suggest that this joining of the particularistic and the temporal in nonobjective art provides us with the main distinction between it and abstract art.

Nonobjective art, then, does not have as its goal a summing-up of nature; rather, it seeks a first incursion into a new aspect of nature's subject matter. The novelty of terrain here, the tentativeness of both symbol-type and field of reference, speaks against formal orthodoxy. The question of permissible form gives way to a question of greater priority: whether the choice of form—be it "a useful article, a heavenly body, or a form materialized by another artist"—is the result, using Kandinsky's term, of "inner necessity." This criterion of inner necessity is more difficult epistemologically than is Mondrian's "pure plastic form."[30] But the threatened circularity in its demonstration can be offset by its theoretical openness to plurality in expressive means. Kandinsky denies that a particular choice of formal elements is taboo in and of itself. To the contrary, he states that any form in present disrepute "is only waiting for its master."[31] Abstract or realist forms, or their combinations, are here all equipotential for an authentic expression. Kandinsky elucidates inner necessity through a critical attack on rule-governed, conventionalized processes—what he calls the "practical-purposeful."[32] In contrast to Mondrian's belief that progress can be evidenced in social collectives—provided that these are "rationalized" through neoplastic principles—Kandinsky locates progress in an individual's rejection of external rules in favor of the primacy of feelings. The art that follows from this he describes as "anarchistic . . . as planfulness and order . . . created by the feeling of the good."[33]

VIII

In the historical context of the theories described here, Mondrian's has the advantage common to objectivist positions: Verification poses little problem, for the theory gives a clear sense of the *characteristic* through an impersonal body of principles and their visual equivalents. This theory of abstraction, though radical in its inceptions, is conservative in its consequences in that it closes itself to further radical transformation. The theory of nonobjective art, as I outline it, relates differently to its past and future. Lacking a program of characteristic form, it offers one of characteristic *sensibility* that employs a negative criterion: verification of the *nonconformity* of its products with each other.[34]

The bemusement with which some view the history of the avant-garde may have to do with these competing claims for the proper characterization of its products. One such claim points to a consistent, progressive, and cumulative purification of "form" evidenced in radical works, and I have identified this as a major component of the theory of abstraction. Another claim emphasizes the achievement of a radicalized aesthetic "consciousness" exemplified by such works, and I equate this version with nonobjective art. The tension between these claims became a major legacy for the programs and procedures of the later avant-garde, that postwar period in American art that is generally accepted as the "successor" style to the European art we have been discussing. In the chapter that follows, I turn to a consideration of this art and to its reformulation of its European legacy into a new but equally contentious array of works and ideologies.

TWO

Kant, "Form," and the Avant-Garde in America

The European phase of the avant-garde came to an end with the advent of World War II. The movement's ideological migration to America and the changes that a new context and a later time produced in both these ideologies and the visual arts supported by them are the subject of this chapter. The history of the avant-garde in Europe, as I discuss in chapters 1 and 3, is marked by a linkage between aesthetic and social concerns. Artworks are seen to exemplify social ideals, personify social criticism, and stir dormant sensibilities. Also, they are seen as doing this through instantiations of "radical" form rather than through "traditional" didactic devices.

In this (European) context, avant-garde art offers its own historical development as a *moral* example to a reluctant social order and thereby indicates that its own achievements are not to be regarded as "merely" aesthetic. In the visual arts, the abstractionist rejection of the representational premises of older art is presented as a *category* change, one that risks the very identity of the enterprise for an ideal of "progress." Societal emulation of this aesthetic risk is then demanded, and its fulfillment requires taking analogous risks in the task of changing the social order.

II

In the later history of the avant-garde, the relationship between radical art and radical sociology is weakened. The movement of avant-garde artists to America was based, in part, on the hope that their ideas would flourish in the new environment. Yet the art that arose here, although undeniably influenced by Europe, was in some respects a rejection of those influences, particularly of the social theses through which the older art justified its formal discoveries.[1] The rise of postwar American art to a position of eminence took a remarkably short time. By 1950, the American avant-garde, its autonomy secured by the new name "abstract expressionism," became the standard of both taste and artistic production. The "art capital of the world," as so many then pointed out, had shifted to New York. Although the journey between continents in the 1940s did not mark the first introduction of twentieth-century radical art to America, its public acceptance at that time coincided with a reinterpretation of its premises. In particular, the thesis of a connecting "obligation" between art and society became a casualty of the journey. The question as to how such an obligation might be fulfilled was replaced by another question: Need radical art have a prescriptive relation to *any* extraaesthetic ideals, or is it essentially "self-justifying"?

In the American context, because the belief in a commonality of interest between radical aesthetic and social ideologies was discarded, differences in aesthetic outlook were no longer interpreted as approximating differences in social outlook. The European "aesthetic utopianism"[2] was a victim not only of the war but of a new postwar agreement on the nature of aesthetic justification. The thesis that obligates art to social ideals is countered, in this later phase, by the thesis that all obligations are self-referential—that art's only obligation is to art. Under this new construal of aesthetic justification, the realm of art is seen as closed and as having no (additional) need for compliants of external reference, whether depictive or critical. Though the influence of the early Hegel is not entirely lost here, its later activist interpretation is discarded. The historical achievement of abstract art is indeed a demonstration of "evolution of spirit," but, once achieved, another basis must be provided for the proper appreciation of spirit's accomplishments. At this point, historicism gives way to formalism, and an emphasis on syntactic self-sufficiency emerges that dissociates art from the issue of progress in society. With this shift a number of new problems arise, but before I discuss these, I want to look more closely at formalism and its sources.

III

Formalism, briefly stated, is the thesis that the value of an artwork lies in the interaction of its phenomenal components independently of any referential (depictive, descriptive) function these components might have. The source of this thesis in Kant's aesthetic theories has often been noted, and later elaborations of the thesis have been used as justifications for much of modern art and particularly for the practice of abstraction.[3] I suggest here that it is in the tension between *discounting* referential characteristics for aesthetic value and *discarding* them from artistic procedure that an important problem is located. It is one thing, for example, to prize representational works for their formal qualities; it is another to prize works because they consist of "nothing but" their formal qualities. This is a problem in interpretation that I call "the persistence of external reference." It arises out of the dictum noted above that avant-garde art is self-referential. One part of the demand here is that works are to be made under a general commitment to principles of abstraction, which serves to ground the inventions of individual artists. The other part is that the works must remain "meaningful," that is, symbolically potent, despite the rejection of any alliance between form and extraartistic ideals. In the first demand, the issue is about the fixing of boundaries between abstract and representational imagery. I discuss this in chapter 1. The second demand—the retention of meaning—is of more immediate concern, for it raises an issue of ontology: how artworks remain *consequentially* art when their referential uniqueness is obscured. This problem arises when we ask whether there are things that we cannot justify as artworks purely on the basis of formalist descriptions.

In answer to this question, we might say that from one standpoint "form" is a ubiquitous characteristic of the physical world—one that is shared by artworks and other sorts of things. In this sense, to attribute form to art is a harmless move, but unfortunately it gives little support in establishing for artworks what, after all, is a wanted credential: uniqueness. Formal differentiation for the sake of establishing artistic identity requires identification of properties that distinguish between, at least, art and nonart and, perhaps, between good and bad art. Such properties are usually chosen because they fit with our reasons for calling the things that possess them "art," and some of these reasons are to be found in our construal of the symbolic function of artworks: what it is they refer to. The notion that an artwork can exhibit a "purely internal" referential pattern is one such reason, and it is usually justified by pointing to abstract art. As persuasive as this notion may seem, however, it is misleading: art is a concept that organizes properties; it is not itself a property. For something to be art, therefore, requires reference to that concept and, by extension, to the conventions that shape it.[4] This is what I mean by "the persistence of external reference." Even within an extreme formalist context, one that rejects representational conventions entirely, the art-making properties of a thing are still to be identified through a referential pattern that establishes an alliance between that thing and a conceptual scheme. This scheme functions to identify certain properties of things as artistic properties and, thereby, provides those things with the ontological status of artwork. Such schemes can themselves be identified through a dominant term which, in turn, is explicated through its "linkage" with other, supporting, terms. This linkage gives us both the substance and the history of that concept. I suggest that "form" is one such dominant term that is in particular conceptual alliance with the American phase of the avant-garde. As I argue above, this term cannot be understood in the context of self-referential properties unless we also know why any such context is "artistic." This knowledge, as I suggest, is provided by the pattern of linkage between form and the terms that are subordinate to it, for these latter provide the values that identify properties as artistic properties. Put another way, this linkage identifies our reasons for wanting certain things to be art.

IV

In order to show how this alliance between form and avant-garde art evolved, I turn to some considerations in the aesthetics of Kant. Although justifications for a formalist position are indeed to be found in the *Critique of Judgment*, there is, within it, an important transition from considerations of the nature of "appreciation" to considerations of the nature of "creativity."[5] I believe that in this transition Kant anticipates the particular alliance between work and theory that characterizes not only nineteenth-century romanticism but the American avant-garde as well. In the "Analytic of the Beautiful," Kant's discussion of the physical characteristics of beauty is rudimentary, but his discussion of its epistemic base is extensive. Apprehension of the world, when it complies with the strictures of the categorical "moments," makes the experience of beauty possible and, perhaps, is the sole ground for affirming its existence. Kant's interest, of course, was in both nature and art. But to adduce beauty of both is not to distinguish between them, nor does it help to locate beauty in form, for both these values remain common to nature and art. The "Aesthetic Judgment," then, does not do the job of distinguishing artworks from other things, for the distinction it makes is between modes of apprehension and not between specific things that are subsumable under one or another mode. But Kant's Judgment *does* make specific reference, not to the world but to a conceptual possibility—that nature is rational. Though nature offers no proof *for* this, natural things can be used as symbols *of* this. Artworks also function this way in that, presumably, they are included here as special kinds of natural things. To call an artwork "natural," particularly in a Kantian context, may seem odd. But to suppose that Kant considered artworks to be, in any important sense, "conventional" is odder still, for it must be remembered that the subject of aesthetic appreciation is an idea of synthesis between realms of thought, and artworks have value here insofar as they function to support the cogency of this idea. The consideration of artworks as natural might be furthered by contemplating how they give such support, and this leads us to a consideration of how they come to be: the question of artistic activity.

In that section of the Third Critique that concerns the "sublime," Kant moves from a discussion of appreciation to one of creativity. Through a distinction analogous to the one he makes earlier between the beautiful and the pleasant, Kant here differentiates between artist and artisan. The distinction, briefly, is between making or "giving" rules and merely following them. The point of interest for my thesis is this: The rule that artists give to their creations is "nature's" rule; it does not originate with the artist. Like Plato's poets "possessed of the gods," Kant's artist is the conduit "through which nature gives the rule to art."[6] Whether or not one takes Kant's statement metaphorically depends, I suppose, on one's estimate of the force of Judgment's synthesis. But that is another problem. "Nature's rules," upon examination, turn out to be peculiar kinds of rules: Although they are "exemplary," they are not meant to be followed by others, nor are they the kind through which we determine, after the fact, if the artist has followed them faithfully and therefore if the created work is "good" or "bad." The codification of these rules does not precede the work but arises simultaneously with its creation. These rules are not exportable; they cannot serve as determinants of other works, for if they did these works would be only "productions" and not the unique creations that are the only proper issue of artist as "genius." Nature's "rule for art," then, is not a rule at all but a symbol of "purposiveness" that is made rather than found—a painting rather than a sunset. Artistic sensibility functions here as a special (compressed) natural process, and an artwork as a special (self-contained) natural kind.

I note above that Kant's artist is artist as "genius," not the ordinary practitioner—only that rara avis that truly fills the role of a "force of nature." Yet we know that the great number of artists are not like this. Must we say, then, that most artistic creations are only artifacts because they are rule-governed and that their makers are only artisans as their efforts are rule-ridden?[7] What these predictable objects and ungifted activities come to in this context is conjectural: Harshly viewed, they have no consequence for Judgment's inquiry, no transcendental import, and are merely "pleasant" objects that may incidentally function as conventional—descriptive or depictive—symbols. Viewed more circumspectly, they could be said to differ in degree, but not in kind, from the creations of genius. Their exemplifications are thus weaker, more diffuse, but are still proper subjects for aesthetic judgment. This second view seems less counterintuitive for modern thought, but it is less plausible as an inference in Kantian aesthetics. His postulate of "genius" seems too radical a conceit to dilute by giving it expression in gradations. The task of the "free play of the imagination" in reconciling the separate issues of Understanding and Reason seems too demanding to be relegated to imaginations that are not adequate, or are not completely adequate, in their capacity to make full use of their "freedom."

One view of Kant's aesthetic theories is that through them he began the nineteenth century's exaltation of art in philosophy by giving (reflective) judgment its high function of synthesizing the separate realms of the First and Second Critiques. A mark of his (perhaps eighteenth-century) caution might be that in the specific aspect of synthesis that involves the creation of art, he restricts the operation of Judgment to those few works of still fewer individuals who have been "given" the capacity of genius. The differences between these views mark the distinction in scope that he makes between "appreciation" and "creation": the capacity for appreciation existing in all individuals, the capacity for creation in only the exceptional few. This is actually a distinction between the categories of "disinterestedness" and "purposiveness" as regards their subject or compliant. I suggest that "disinterestedness," because it governs the refining of attitude, applies primarily to "appreciation," and "purposiveness," because it identifies a special coherence of relationships, governs form. In comparing the two, we see that the capacity for appreciation is widespread. It is an acquired capacity consonant with moral development, which requires a recognition of the implications of natural beauty. This recognition, in turn, is supported by a motive-neutral, "disinterested" perception. On the other hand, the creative capacity is exclusive, a "gift"—unsolicited—to genius. The created work is purposive in the sense that it symbolizes the unlimited expanse of harmony and coherence in nature through an artifact that has specific limits. These are limits not only of the physical vehicle but of the symbol—the artistic "world" presented as coherent form. The achievement of genius is in the compression of natural purposiveness into artifactual purposiveness. In this way, nature's significance as a symbol of rationality is transferred, in form, to the work of art.

v

I return now to my concern with the relation between formalist theory and avant-garde art. My discussion above of formalist roots in Kantian aesthetics identifies a number of ways in which this relationship can be examined. One way is to follow Kant and begin with the following hypothesis: Only that form is truly artistic which is the issue of genius. In the search for the values that join with form to compose the ideological alliance of the late avant-garde, it might be well to follow the fortunes of genius into the twentieth century. If we think back to the period between the two world wars and to the art-critical terminology then in use, one of the major valuational terms undoubtedly was "creativity." It was used as a justification of both artworks and artistic acts. Indeed, part of its strength—and popularity—derives precisely from the closeness it imparts to works and acts, a closeness that tends to discourage consideration of each in separate terms. My hypothesis of the inferential relationship between the terms "form" and "genius" can be modified by replacing these terms with the analogous although more contemporary terms "artwork" and "creative act" without denying the Kantian derivation. For either set of terms, the basic issue remains the same: A special kind of (creating) activity justifies our construal of the created object as a special (artistic) kind. However, the historical span between genius and creativity creates contextual differences of some importance, differences that show why creativity—but not genius—is acceptable as a value in the avant-garde. The most evident difference is that creativity, in this period, is not consequentially restricted to genius but is seen as a general characteristic of human activity that occurs in a concentrated and/or specialized form in artistic activity. This catholicity dilutes the notion of genius both as regards the philosophical task that Kant assigns it and, on a more mundane level, as a sufficient reason for the practice of art-making.

In the historical development of modernism, creativity in its new role as a constituent of general practice comes to supplant the more restrictive notion of genius as a justification for art. One can surmise that the importance of genius wanes when the notion that art provides a special kind of knowledge about the world is brought into question. Kant, as we know, restricted the knowledge claim of reflective judgment through an "as-if" clause. Later nineteenth-century philosophers (e.g., Hegel and Schopenhauer) were more prolix in this regard, and art became the instrument of choice for probing the "inner" or "essential" workings of reality. Genius, going beyond Kant's usage, provided the force for this high—and exclusive—purpose. The deflation of these theories in twentieth-century philosophy also worked to deny to art its instrumentality for extraempirical knowledge. With this change, genius lost its identity as a separate faculty—its "in-kind" distinction—and simply became one of the terminal values on a scale of relative ability. The value of creativity, once seen as coextensive with genius, became a measure of *degree* of achievement and was incrementally distributed along the entire range of that scale.

The alliance between genius and knowledge, then, once dissolved, led to the emancipation of creativity from genius. A curious inversion of Kant's aesthetic values occurs here. For him, genius is the rare unteachable capacity possessed by only a few, whereas the capacity for appreciation is open to and attainable by all. In the transition from the value of genius to that of creativity, however, the latter comes to take on the ubiquity of appreciation. We are all, for example, "creative"; we need only to free ourselves from the psychological constraints that "inhibit" us. Now, we notice that this requirement is analogous to one Kant has for aesthetic appreciation: We are all capable of experiencing "beauty"; we need only put aside the "practical," goal-directed constraints that limit our usual sense of the world. Thus creativity, a requirement of art-making, becomes as commonplace as the capacity for appreciation.[8]

As artworks lost their philosophical "exclusivity" in the course of modernism, there seemed no overwhelming reason to restrict one condition of their making—creativity—solely to them. This term came to apply to any activity requiring a modicum of skill and imagination, and thus its role in affirming the special nature of artworks was weakened. Evidently, other values were needed to reaffirm that special nature, values that would not merely specify form within artworks but would link them to a consequential belief about the world. In chapter 1, I identify one such value as the ideal of social progress, and in this chapter I indicate that this characteristic alliance of the European avant-garde did not survive the transition to America. When the linkage between form and social ideals failed in the context of the American avant-garde, the renewed isolation of form bespoke the need to build a new conceptual alliance. The historical solution to this need, in fact, was a rapprochement between form and a value that exceeds even creativity as a commonplace in contexts of use: self-expression.

The term "self-expression" is actually very much like "form" in that both are ubiquitous in their respective realms of application. In my discussion above I note the various alliances that function to delimit form within the ontological category of artwork. A similar move is needed here to delimit self-expression, for, taken in one sense, this term ranges too broadly to be of use in justifications of art or, for that matter, of any other activity. It could be argued, for example, that all human actions are self-expressive. One might ask here why this term need be introduced at all when its predecessor, "creativity," is already too extended for the task of specifying artworks. The answer is that self-expression is the quintessentially democratic value, which in its exercise implies no special ability and in its result no special distinction. To call it a value at all is perhaps only to distinguish between open and repressed psychological states, to affirm the mere possibility of function; but it is not to suggest the potential for use in critical judgment. In fact, self-expression is anticritical for aesthetic contexts in that its mere application to the class of artworks neither distinguishes nor generates values for instances of that class. The value of self-expression is to be found in its occurrences, not in its products. Works may testify to and "embody" these occurrences, but (formal) differences between products should not be taken as indicating levels of success in self-expression.

The aesthetic value of "expression," when conjoined with "self," is parasitic on the ethical value that we assign to selves, namely, that they are all equal. Ignoring the category mistake permits the conclusion that all instances of self-expression are equally valuable. Of course, it is possible to extract "covert" judgements from artworks because, as testimonials, works might tell us when a self has "truly" been expressed. But, then, evidence of such success must include the formal properties of the works at issue, and we are again at the question of what these formal properties are like. Answers to this question establish a link between self-expression and form that relegates creativity to the historical past. We may hold that, to express a self, no special (creative) ability is required; but, then, a distinction of *some* kind is still wanted, for otherwise we would be left with no value at all.

Justifications of artistic style often make use of metaphor when they are used polemically. In this context of the American avant-garde, the literal sense of "self-expression" is given a metaphorical interpretation in which the "valuelessness" of self-expression itself becomes a value. When we examine this metaphor, we find a series of denials that is aimed not only at "traditional" art but at the European avant-garde. The substance of these denials is that skill, conception, product, have no essential relevance to the practice of art. I suggest that interpreting self-expression through these denials leads to the positive programs of American avant-garde art and also indicates why that ideology was so successful in its rapid expansion into general culture. It would seem, offhand, that to deny skill, conception, and product is effectively to leave no grounds for making art and no reason for its appreciation. But it must be remembered that American art, for all of its debts to its European predecessor, was also a reaction against the latter's "high seriousness." These "denials" can be understood as polemical forms of that reaction, meant to cast doubt on past achievements and thus to provide impetus for new ones.

When we consider the programs of such European artists as Mondrian, Kandinsky, and Malevich, we find other denials leveled at their own antecedents for similar polemical reasons.[9] These are worth reviewing before we go on to discuss the later period. One denial found in European avant-garde ideology rejects "painterly" skills in favor of "analytic" ones and locates the critical difference between the two in the presumption that an analytic or "constructivist" technique does not require virtuosity. This denial also suggests that an adequate technique is not to be found in academic training; indeed, the best technique is seen as "no technique" in that the austerity of the enterprise demands a directness and "honesty" of application that academically habituated artists do not achieve. The openness implied here is deceptive, however, for although skill is freed from academic constraints it is bound in another way by its subordination to concept. These European artists, as I discuss in chapter 1, are concerned with a precise presentation of certain programmatic—social and philosophical—values through art. These values are programmatic in the sense that their formulation precedes their "embodiment" in works. Skill is the method that presents these values most clearly. In this context, the demands of the conception limit the acts that give it concrete form to just those fitting *that* conception and no other. There is no symbiosis here between conception and skill such that the latter could modify the former through the suggestiveness of an improvisation—or a happy accident. To be sure, there are differences between the programs of the artists I refer to: Mondrian is concerned with the historical purification of form whereas Kandinsky's preoccupation is with personal "spiritual" purification. But these are differences of emphasis within a larger context of rationalistic ideology, and the point here is that the notion of skill is both limited and made explicit by reference to that ideology. The product, in this context the "artwork," is interpreted through the denial that it is either a picture or a commodity. The search for purity in form leads inexorably to an art of abstraction, whereas the accomplishments of spirit entail a critique of material—social—excess. These accomplishments deny to the audience the satisfactions of pictorial illusionism and painterly virtuosity and, by extension, criticize its society for wanting either.

VI

The American avant-garde, for its own reasons, denied the European denials not by discarding them but by inverting them. In this way the historical pattern of "radicality" could be continued but its European legacy minimized. I now take up two versions of this "inversion" as they are exemplified by the works of the American artists Jackson Pollock and Ad Reinhardt. Although both artists are historically identified with abstract expressionism, their works stand in considerable contrast to one another. Indeed, this contrast seems much greater than that between Kandinsky and Mondrian, and in the case of Reinhardt the affinity seems much closer with Mondrian than with Pollock. Notwithstanding, I argue that the two American artists have in

Jackson Pollock, *Number 1, 1948* (1948). Oil on canvas, 68 × 8'8".
Collection, The Museum of Modern Art, New York. Purchase.

common their rejections of European social ideology through an ideal of self-expression, even though the sense of these rejections—like that of their work—is very different. I begin my discussion with Pollock because, of the two, his work is more identified with the popular image of abstract expressionism and has become a standard for both the uniqueness and the value of American postwar art. [10]

Above, I identify the American polemics leveled at the European avant-garde as a series of denials, namely, the denials that skill, concept, and product are consequential for artistic activity. In Jackson Pollock's work, the denial of skill becomes an affirmation of action: the forming act that is unfettered by any prior formal objective. Such acts need not be examples of established artistic practice, however, much less good examples. In this context, there no longer are acts that "belong to" painting, or sculpture, in the same sense that there no longer are particular painterly or sculptural materials. The realms themselves are not yet threatened—that belongs to a later time[11]—but each habituated practice of a realm becomes a target for a new denial.

Concept, here, is seen as a formal objective which is denied priority and loses coherence through its identification with process. As process is the immediacy of the moment sustained through an indefinite—although finite—duration of moments, coherence of concept is regained through inspection of the outcome. As this occurs after the fact of the work, however, it plays no role in the formation of that work. The parameters of the canvas, which heretofore had circumscribed the "world" of the work, expand in scale and become the "field" of the artist's action. Denied its formal self-sufficiency, this expanded work may function as an environment in which the spectator's "appreciation" occurs through self-inclusion, or the work may appear as a stage in which the "tracks" of the painterly process are observed and followed because they are evidence that the artist's self is well and truly expressed. Pollock's method of painting on a horizontally placed canvas insures that he remains close to its surface as he moves across its expanse. While his relationship to the canvas is thus intimate and "physical," it is also partial and fragmentary. The surface is worked until a certain density of paint and velocity of form are reached.

The denial of "composition" occurs through the achievement of a surface that is sufficiently concrete and active to reflect the painting process directly. The imperatives of balance, proportion, and so forth, that remain virtues for the European avant-garde are here denied because the painting is not placed upright (i.e., "distanced," seen as a "whole") until after it is complete. The formal virtue that is looked for here is "flatness," and its usual interpretation is that the painted surface is of the sort that does not lend itself to illusionistic interpretation. Because the physical act of painting consists of laying down pigment on a two-dimensional surface, so the perception of that surface should corroborate the nature of that act by interpreting the visual forms two-dimensionally. The "should" in the second clause identifies this equation as normative for, indeed, while it is impossible to *eliminate* spatial clues in any given configuration, it is possible to *discount* them. Through this discounting of illusionistic readings, the "integrity" of the artist's act—and, hence, of his self—becomes the paramount value in the work. Often, when Pollock's paintings are on display in large museum spaces, they seem—seen from a distance—to be illusionistic evocations of a generalized landscape.[12] So represented, they misrepresent their formative act by being conventionalized into "pictures." There are, of course, no overwhelming reasons why artists' acts need to be taken into account in appreciation. But when ideological value, as in this case, is located primarily in painterly process and only residually in its products, then taking a Pollock as a picture becomes an oblique justification of the denial, cited above, that the product constitutes an artistic value. This discrepancy between the artistic act and its public use, in the European context, would have been interpreted as yet another reason for

Ad Reinhardt. *Abstract Painting* (1960–61). Oil on canvas, 60 × 60".
Collection, The Museum of Modern Art, New York. Purchase by exchange.

social criticism. As it was, the matter was regarded with indifference, an indication of the transfer of value, in American art, from the collective to the self.

The work of Ad Reinhardt,[13] for a number of reasons, is often more closely identified with European geometric abstraction than with American art. There are the apparent—and, as I shall argue, deceptive—formal similarities. Then, too, there is Reinhardt's prolific theoretical work, a preoccupation quite common among European artists but rare among Americans. Actually, to include Reinhardt among the abstract expressionists is to do some disservice to both his polemics and his personal history, for he was

a gadfly and critic who disparaged the "cult of self" that he attributed to
Pollock, de Kooning, and others. Yet the substance of his attacks as well as
his own work point away from European solutions into quite a new realm.
Within this realm, his value of "selflessness" and its correlate, "art as art,"
establish the polar opposites to the values through which I discuss the art of
Pollock. Taken together, these two sets of values indicate the "shape" of the
ideology I attribute to the American avant-garde. I discuss Reinhardt's work
through the same series of denials I apply above to Pollock: the denials that
skill, concept, and product are necessary ingredients in artistic value.

To paint uniformly colored, symmetrically arranged, rectilinear planes
"freehand" is not the only—perhaps not the best—way to paint them. If
one places no pictorial value on the small discrepancies in edge and surface
that inhere in this method, then insisting—as Reinhardt did—that no such
mechanical devices as masking tape are appropriate reveals a concern with
some extrapictorial value. If skill in this context is precision, and the most
conscientious hand remains imprecise, then the effort to do what cannot be
done exposes the pretense that skill is at all an avenue to what is valuable.
Mondrian worked out his compositions through various stages of collage
and, when he was satisfied, placed the canvas flat and laid in his colors. He
stated that he "enjoyed" that effort, presumably as a sensual pleasure hark-
ing back to his earlier work—a small gratification softening his present
austerity. [14] For Reinhardt, the painting part was not gratifying; it was more
like a penance—perhaps for being (historically) late. The painting part was,
in fact, "impossible," but then, *painting* had become impossible. However,
the time for confronting impossibility was now; all was not over yet, and one
did what one had to do. What Reinhardt "had to do" was not new—nor
"his"—it was the "same old thing," a Parmenidean constancy of art "as
art." One could protest here that the image of a barely visible, repetitive,
black cruciform *is* new—whatever else it might be. But Reinhardt's newness is closed in that he is arguably the first to assert that he is painting
"the last paintings that could be painted" [15]—although both Mondrian and
Malevich suggest as much. On this issue Reinhardt is closer to Schopenhauer than to Hegel, for the "last painting" is not that optimistic herald
of the emergence of a more "potent" symbol, a symbol adequate to the
demands of a more comprehensive level of "idea." Rather, it is a reaction
both pessimistic and dispassionate to the victory of time over achievement,
and a gesture of autonomy that rejects the popular conflation of self with
either novelty or catharsis. This reaction does not constitute an abnegation of
self, however, except perhaps in the Zen sense that interested Reinhardt: to
lose one's self is a way toward finding it. To stand patiently before the still
paintings until the cruciform emerges is, perhaps, a propaedeutic for the task

of finding a self. Reinhardt's paintings are neither environment nor theater; they exist quietly within the bounds of their format. They are neither active, visible, nor different one from the other. They are, paradoxically, each the universal to which they all, as instances, belong. They do function critically, somewhat in the European sense, in that they trivialize the desire for uniqueness and the need for comparison upon which acquisition of art is typically based.

In his writings, teaching, and public lectures, Reinhardt was an inveterate critic of the mores of the artworld. He insisted, however, as he did about his own paintings, that these criticisms were "impersonal," that they were leveled at those practices—art-making as "theater," the artist as "hero," collecting for "social status"—that he considered to be "antiart." However, unlike Mondrian, Reinhardt offered no program through which such practices could be overcome. Even his own work was of no help here for, after all, it exemplified an end, and only the singular self who reaches an end can paint its image over and over again—in the same way. For the rest of us, I believe that Reinhardt held out the (aesthetic) possibility of not—or no longer—making art. Some might complain that, in this, he conflates aesthetic and ethical values; Reinhardt might have replied that these are the same. We may remember that Pollock, in his later work, rejected the solution of "silence" and sought a way out of the impasse of his own repetitions by taking on figurative motifs. We may also remember that Kandinsky thought this a perfectly good move—when supported by a "pure consciousness." Reinhardt would have disagreed.

Kant states, in the "Transcendental Logic," that concepts without percepts are empty and percepts without concepts are blind.[16] In this way he denies the possibility of independent function to either. Taken as metaphors of self for the discussion of Pollock and Reinhardt, however, "blindness" and "emptiness" can stand, respectively, as goals of their artistic efforts and thus exist as possibilities or ideals. "Pure act" is blind in the sense that, ideally, it denies the need to stop and see how things are. The ideal of "pure form" is empty because it excludes all traces of the time of its making and, in this sense, never starts. Of course, Pollock and Reinhardt did not achieve these ideals for, given all else, they still made objects. But I suggest that these terms can be taken as fairly precise metaphors for the subjects of their work.

At this point the familiar (but not always welcome) call for "synthesis" must be faced. Why, after all, do my exemplars of the American avant-garde occupy extreme rather than median positions in the relevant ideology? Although at bottom, I suppose, it comes to my own tastes, there are other reasons as well. I think that synthesis in art is less valuable than synthesis in epistemology: Although the claim for the possibility of knowledge is undoubtedly strengthened by intersecting concept and percept, an art that is half-empty and half-blind may only be one that is impure and partially free. My choice of Pollock and Reinhardt as parameters of the American avant-garde is based on the singularity of their positions and on the clarity of focus through which their particular denials of European avant-garde values transform into the values they adopt. The process of conceptual linkage through which I describe these transformations does not end at this point, however. The "end of art" that is suggested by Pollock and Reinhardt remains a metaphor, one that is vulnerable to other values—a new linkage. In the chapters that follow, I discuss some of these.

Adorno, "Protest," and the Twelve-Tone Row

Theodor Adorno's view of the development of modern music is both apocalyptic and pessimistic. As a witness to the social crises of the early twentieth century, he locates analogous crises in twentieth-century music. He correlates the two through a thesis of historical discontinuity wherein "modernism" contrasts with its own—"traditional"—past in certain essential ways.[1] The tensions that Adorno develops in his subject are mirrored in his style: Assertions given are immediately taken away and turned on their backs. This has been criticized as jargon; it can also be defended as "nonsuppression of antagonisms," a Hegelian virtue usually assigned to the free operation of a social dialectic. Either way, Adorno is an easy target for criticism of an "analytic" sort. But he is, after all, a major theorist of the avantgarde and, if one is concerned with the art at issue, it seems to me more important to circle about his underlying beliefs than to spear them straightaway for their inconsistencies, arrogances, or whatever. This is probably what Heidegger meant by "understanding," and it seems a good way—one that I take—to understand Adorno.

The "evolutionary" theory of historical change, for Adorno, is inadequate sociology because he sees the twentieth century, by and large, as constituting a betrayal of the earlier ideals of personal freedom and political equality. Equally, the thesis of formal continuity in music is inadequate aesthetics because modern music, in reaction to its own social matrix, breaks that continuity by taking on the function of criticism. The valuable work of older—traditional—music is accounted a "masterwork," which signifies a certain accessibility of the work to its social institutions through performance and appreciation. For Adorno there can be no masterpieces in twentieth-century music because the imperative of criticism or protest inhibits accessibility and fosters alienation. Thus, the valuable modern work is counted a "radical work," one that confounds the received practices of appreciation, yet one that exemplifies the most advanced historical development of musical form.[2]

One distinction between Adorno's thesis and the garden varieties of social realism is that Adorno tries to reconcile radical sociology and radical music, and thereby challenges both purely formalist and purely instrumentalist aesthetics. For him, the value of music is to be found both in its innovational achievements and in its utility for social change, or—at least—social "witness." Radical music is seen to omit the devices of integration properly characteristic of traditional works—although improper for modern works—and the consequence is that radical music is doomed to remain largely unheard. However, Adorno views this not as simply an unfortunate historical happenstance but rather as a deliberate artistic choice, perhaps the only choice that preserves the autonomy of musical form while it supports the stance of protest. Radical music protests precisely through its inaccessibility—its not being heard. In his analysis, Adorno's musical polemics are supported by his social polemics. My question here is essentially how the latter are exhibited in the former. In my discussion I do not analyze Adorno's sociology; I accept it as a given and ask only how the music he champions can be understood to exemplify his attacks on bourgeois society. For my thesis, it does not matter whether Adorno's criticism of modern society is cogent, for here I wish to indicate a link between a particular normative content and a particular musical form.

Adorno's heroes, as is well known, are Schoenberg, Berg, Webern—the principal early exponents of atonal, or "dodecaphonic," music.[3] The direct paths to this music are found, importantly, in the preatonal, "expressionist" works of these same composers and in the developments of nineteenth-century music, primarily of Beethoven, Wagner, Brahms, Mahler, with Beethoven cast as the primary exemplar of a music that, for a fleeting historical moment, is both autonomous and accessible. I shall not, here, pay much attention to Adorno's villains: Stravinsky, Hindemith, et al., or to an analysis of what constitutes musical villainy except in the obvious sense that it involves a rejection of Adorno's tenets for musical value.

My principal aim is to locate the critical function in atonal music, that is, where, structurally, "protest" occurs and how it is manifested. Adorno says much about this, but it remains elusive. He does not say what I eventually come to say, although I feel that he implies (at least some of) what I say.

Accordingly, this chapter should be viewed not as a general exposition of Adorno's aesthetics but rather as my analysis of a particular issue he has set before us: one juncture, both aesthetic and normative, between artistic form and social theory. Adorno discusses the inaccessibility of radical music primarily in terms of its social "fate"—the dearth of performances and the indifference of audiences. But there is a problem here: The fate described is not unique to radical music; it is suffered by all obscure works—of whatever kind. More importantly, this account identifies only the negative factor of social avoidance and does not tell us what positive, or "adequate," appreciation would be like. Evidently we need to know this if we are to ascertain the fact of musical protest and come to recognize specific instances of the music at issue.

My own thesis in this regard can be stated as follows: the radical music of which Adorno speaks is inaccessible because it is *inaudible*. I define inaudibility as a particular relation between the twelve-tone row as it is constituted in the score and the score as it is performed. I hold that adequate appreciation here cannot be limited to the performance but must include certain non-sensuous aspects of the score. The listener is enjoined to refer the auditory event to the notational deployment of the row. However, the requirements for such reference exceed what can be ascertained through listening, and, therefore, adequate appreciation for such music presupposes data and beliefs that are come by in other ways. The protest function in radical music is to be found in this restructuring of appreciation and in the concomitant social insights it provides.

II

Before I proceed to develop my "inaudibility" thesis through a more detailed discussion of dodecaphonic music, I will first look at some ordinary uses of this term and thereby develop certain differentia between the concepts: "traditional" and "radical." Common sense would indicate that for music to be appreciable it should be audible. It could thus keep good company with "visible" visual art and "legible" literature. Nothing tricky here, only the claim that the sensuous vehicle is a sufficient condition for the aesthetic experience. Music, prima facie, seems to fit this claim better than do its companions: The visual arts, although sensuous, elude being vehicles insofar as they are nonnotational;[4] literature, on the other hand, locates its sensuousness not in the script but in the imagination. Perhaps this is what prompted Hegel to give music the middle position in romantic art.[5]

Music, as it is both sensuous and mediated, should manifest a linkage between these two aspects. Accordingly, we consider the sounds we hear in performance to be referents of the score, although we also know that only some of the performance characteristics are specified by that reference. The reverse of this—whether we hear what is in the score—translates easily into a question of value: whether we should hear all that is written. It would seem, offhand, that if we did not hear what the score contains, either the music has failed or we did not listen closely enough. "Musical failure," here, might be taken as a matter of the composer's ineptness: a score so conceived that some of it, under accepted standards of reference and acuity, cannot be distinguished as a sound-event. However, I will argue, apropos "radical" music, that this is not to be regarded as a failure because, in such music, scores maintain a unique independence—both formal and valuational— from their performances.

Failure to hear can also be blamed on the performance, that some part of the score was played incorrectly, although, on some such occasion, we might like what we did hear. Correct performances of the same work differentiate by emphasizing certain aspects of the score and obscuring others so that, of the aspects that are audible, we only attend to some. Conductors occasionally claim (less these days) that they perform works as these were "originally" scored—or "intended." But such claims do not easily sustain belief, for they each come to be seen as an instance of one conductor revising another's emphasis. So the notion of "paradigm performance" crumbles, and new versions of familiar works continue to proliferate. Radical music, however, is less susceptible to variations in performance, for its appreciation—as I claim—is not entirely vested in listening. One expected consequence of this is that such music is infrequently played. I will argue that this expectation contributes to a criticism of the music's social matrix.

Another "failure to hear" can be blamed on us—the audience. We defeat audibility in any number of ways: when we hum along as we dine or inter-weave the music with images of lovers, voyages, or childhood sorrows. We may, in defense, blame the music—some works in particular—for being seductive on this score although we might also admit that resisting such seductions is a way to a more adequate appreciation. One need not hold for this view that hummable and image-evoking music must be bad, only that, if worthwhile, it invariably is historical and, therefore, not free of performing a "service" role within its society. This suggests that modern radical music, because it has "finally" achieved autonomy,[6] is subject to no extramusical limitations to its formal ambitions. Our awareness of this historical achievement teaches us to listen within earlier music for the autonomy—the formal self-sufficiency—that there remains covert.

On two counts this thesis fits well into the Hegelian framework of Adorno's aesthetics: (1) Music is one with other social forms in the "urge" to historical progress, that is, the "evolution of spirit" from external imposition to self-determination of "freedom." In this sense, musical works, taken together with these other forms, have relative—historical— value. (2) Music is viewed through a purely internal tradition of master works in which the possibilities of musical form evolve but the degree to which each level of possibility is realized remains fixed within each period or "style." In this sense, musical works have absolute value independently of their historical position. On two other counts, however, this thesis departs from its Hegelian roots: (3) In Hegel, the quest for autonomy shows a series of historical approximations. Its full achievement, though not assigned the status of a Kantian "regulatory ideal," is, nevertheless, historically remote. Adorno's construal of modern radical music indicates that it is now fully— and finally—free of the social impositions and formal restrictions connected with music's contribution to other (nonmusical) social functions. (4) Within the Hegelian dialectic, the quest for autonomy is relativized by the demands of new, "purified" content. Within this process, art forms achieve dominance and then fade in the course of history. But each demise is also a success; it augurs a new beginning and is a cause for philosophical optimism. Adorno's construal of radical music, however, indicates that it achieves autonomy at a quite un-Hegelian price. "Success," here, produces not a further continuity but, rather, a historical stasis and alienation. New music is not, in its turn, gracefully superseded; it is shunned.

I have thus far construed the notion of inaudibility as evidence of either compositional ineptness or appreciative failure. But now, if we follow Adorno's "historical discontinuity" view of both modern art and modern society, inaudibility takes on a very different meaning.

Traditional music performs social service in specific ways—for example, through its role in church liturgy, in celebrations of nationalism, in court and salon affairs, in festivals. The inability to appreciate such music typically marks some individual deficiency—for example, in birthright, education, wealth, religious or political persuasion. Aesthetic appreciation, in this context, functions as an arbiter of background, taste, and influence. Failure to appreciate indicates an inability to understand the uses of what one hears and, by extension, an inability to function in the social milieu for which these works were made. As such failures in appreciation are noted by those who succeed, this points to the alliance, in a traditional context, between the arts and social status and to the role of the arts in the preservation of social institutions. Appreciation, here, is in the service of the dominant social class, and its exercise serves to clarify and support rather than to undermine this class.

The role of music in contemporary culture is conceived very differently when we follow Adorno's argument. The general premise of discontinuity between modernism and the past can be specified in the late bourgeois "betrayal" of romanticism. When Adorno refers to music as an "essentially bourgeois art,"[7] he refers specifically to music from Beethoven on—that is, to music whose development parallels the rise of the Western democracies. The specific parallel is between the possibilities of social freedom and musical autonomy. The actuality, as Adorno describes it, is the failure of continuing social transformation: the failure to achieve Marxist-utopian social ideals, the ensuing degeneration of bourgeois culture, and the rise of totalitarian states. Music, in a certain sense, fares better here than does society, for although the forces of musical decadence and trivialization are over-whelming, yet the achievements of Schoenberg and his group do fulfill the possibilities implicit in early romanticism. However, as I note above, this achievement has a cost. The growing disparity between social and musical development couples formal freedom with social alienation. Within its development music discards its traditional service function, yet it is unable to assume a new symbiotic relation with its culture. The only social role left to music that is compatible with autonomy is the one of criticism. By virtue of the demands its appreciation makes upon the listener, music strives to destroy society's illusions and to present it with its actual face. This coupling of autonomy and criticism transforms new music into radical music. Further, it furnishes the value criteria that distinguish radical works from other new works, those that through regressive devices (e.g., "neoclassicism," "mannerism") avoid the critical task.

What are these "demands of appreciation" imposed by radical music, and what relation do they have to the music's formal properties? I describe Adorno's view of musical history as at once discontinuous and apocalyptic: A formal teleology is realized, and a social irrelevance is suffered. If music's formal victory is thus rendered hollow by society's indifference, adequate appreciation of such music must itself be compensatory to this indifference. It must be an act more austere, perhaps more aggressive, than we have tradi-tionally understood appreciation to be. When we view appreciation as an "enjoyable" experience, we usually presume a link between such enjoyment and certain properties of the subject—for example, wholeness, harmonious articulation of parts, satisfactory resolution of development. In this frame-work, the experience is counted as most desirable—perhaps most "aes-thetic"—when the descriptions of its subject also serve to describe the affective state of the audience. Whatever "harmony," "wholeness," "satisfaction," are taken to mean when applied to the *qualities* of things or events, these terms are seen as—at least—analogously descriptive of the *experiences* of such things or events.

But this is familiar territory, so I now move directly to the hypothesis that, in general, this sense of appreciation accords primarily with those historical periods in which music has both a service and a musical function, when it is designed to ingratiate as it unfolds.[8] Inadequate appreciation, in this context, occurs when the service function is mistaken as the paramount one. It is here that Adorno finds the seeds of radical protest. Traditional music performs a covert criticism when its listeners succumb to the temptation of luxuriating solely in the ongoing present, when they engage in purely linear listening because they are seduced by the apparent familiarity and predictability of the harmonic and melodic sequences. Failure to resist such temptation makes for indiscriminate appreciation because what is then experienced is typical surface rather than unique structure. A more adequate appreciation of such music entails, however, not a puritanical disavowal of enjoyment but, rather, its "going through."[9] Such deeper appreciation requires that enjoyment of sequence be coupled with "spatial" understanding, that is, a grasp of the music's "shape," where experience of the musical event configurates across, as well as within, the flow of time. This requirement is analogous to a silent reading of the score where one may skip pages, return to beginnings, and preview conclusions.

But few of us—however accomplished—would wish to confine appreciation to perusals of scores. Obviously, a performance satisfies more than "music in the mind."[10] We require performances, we say, because music is *underdetermined* by its score, and we point to the constitutive nonnotational differences between performances. Though this assertion is usually meant to include all music—traditional and modern—I will argue that in a special sense Adorno's radical music is *overdetermined* by the score and that this alters the requirements for its appreciation. But first I would like to pursue the underdetermination thesis a bit further.

The service function I take as a characteristic of traditional music is indicated, in part, by the music's accessibility, at some level of appreciation, to the most unsophisticated listener. Another indicator of traditional structure is the importance of differences between performances. The performer can be seen here as a mediator between the "self-sufficiency" of the score and the listener's need for gratification. The performer makes the score accessible not only by giving a sensory specification of the notational elements but also by adding to them, "socializing" them, with the nonscored liberties of interpretation. The continuing attractions of multiple performances of traditional music are a mainstay of our concert halls and recording industry. This, in itself, attests to the importance for the appreciation of such works, of the differences between their performances.

In listening to traditional music, we assume that all the notational properties of the score are semantic properties—specifically, that the compliant is the performance we hear. It may be exceedingly difficult in large-scale orchestral music to discriminate all atomic compliants, that is, the individual sounds of all scored notes. But we consider these to be indirectly audible in the sense that they contribute to the sonority of the whole; we presume that their absence, upon repeated listenings, would come to be noticed.[11] We take this as a challenge to our own acuity, and also as showing that differences between performances occur through emphasis on different aspects of the score. However, we would clearly distinguish between a deemphasized note and an unplayed note because we would want to maintain—for any correct performance—the possibility that every scored note can be heard. This promise of audibility places adequate appreciation entirely in the auditory event. Of course, there are other things we may want to know about the work that we find in other places (e.g., analyses, historical and biographical data, etc.). But such things we count as either irrelevant to appreciation per se or as helping us to appreciate the work by directing our attention to what there is to hear.

III

I propose now that this description of appreciation, which is appropriate to the context of traditional music, must be modified for Adorno's category of modern radical music because there appreciation is not entirely located in the auditory event. Adorno accuses his society of rejecting a dialectically feasible—historically achievable—ideal in favor of a retrogression to specialized sectarian interests. Yet this "decadent" society, in striving to project an illusion of coherence, takes as its own analogue the antiquarian forms of traditional music. Accordingly, its adherents reject as "meaningless" or "unenjoyable"[12] the modes of experience that would be adequate to the forms of new—radical—music. Although radical music exemplifies the furthest evolution of musical form, its social matrix testifies to a historical failure. It is this failure that a successful appreciation of radical music purports to reveal.

A more detailed account of radical form and its appreciation is now needed. Adorno indicates that between the received array of syntactic elements—the "system" of notation—and the procedure of composing lies another procedure: the choice and design of a twelve-tone row. He describes this design as "a preliminary study by the composer . . . before the actual composition begins" and continues: "Music becomes the result of processes to which the materials of music have been subjected and the perception of which in themselves is blocked by the music." He says further that "the compositional process actually begins only when the ordering of the twelve tones is established."[13] The choice of a row, then, is not arbitrary but is nevertheless an activity distinct from the composition of a particular piece. The "same" row may underlie a number of different compositions, yet the musical work, once complete, includes both the formulated row and the composed piece upon which it is based. The strictures the row places upon the music are, by now, familiar—for example, the requirement that every tone of the row be sounded in sequence before any can be returned to. Despite these strictures, however, the differences between pieces based upon the same row may be extremely complex and rich, for each row is interpreted through only some of its possible variations within a given composition.[14] The elaboration of a row into its variants—unlike the choice of row itself—need not occur prior to composition, but, nevertheless, each variant is linked through a logical derivation to the original row. The rigor of this derivation, as with the design of the row, is independent of the compositional activity where the row and its variants are deployed. I observe here that the formulation of the row and the derivations of its variants are musical but not auditory events in that they are not retrievable from the performed piece. More precisely, these "logical" events are aspects of the syntax of the work that do not have auditory compliants in the work as sound-event.

Adorno describes dodecaphonic (consistently twelve-tone) music as polyphonic in structure. This indicates that each horizontal sequence is a particular exposition of a chosen row but that no exposition is modified for the sake of the character of the vertical clusters, that is, the "chords" that are formed by the parallel nature of these sequences. In the hierarchic structure of traditional harmony, elements differ in both structural and auditory value. Not all elements are part of coherent horizontal developments; some arise in particular places simply as contributions to the sonority of a vertical, chordal progression. That such elements may not individually be noticed seems perfectly in accord with their service function, which is the support and elaboration of the principal themes.

In modern polyphony, however, there are no principal themes; Adorno denies that there are any themes at all.[15] All horizontal sequences are self-sufficient, and each musical element is autonomous in that it functions primarily in the development of the sequence to which it belongs. This presumption of autonomy rests on the rule that the occurrence of a note is justified not primarily by reference to sensibility but by its place in the exposition of a row. Sensibility is not, thereby, rendered obsolete in this type of music, but its exercise is contingent upon the compatibility of any given choice of note with the row's systematic exposition.

If music conceived in this way were located entirely in the sound-event, one would expect the greatest transparency in texture so that each element of each row could be precisely heard. One would also expect the greatest clarity in shape so that the exposition of each row could be followed in its entirety.

Yet we know that in paradigm examples of atonal music these expectations are often not met. In some works, multiple sequences develop simultaneously, and the dynamics of their orchestration create dense textures in which the identities of particular notes are masked. In other works, the expositions of rows occur in vastly different time frames, some in quick runs that are on the extreme edge of distinctness, others in prolonged passages that undermine the span of attention. In still other works, the variations on a row may be so numerous and complexly stated that they escape identification, and, consequently, the shape of their exposition is not perceived.[16]

When we consider these and other auditory characteristics of dodecaphonic works, we find a disjunction between performance and score that seems willful in its thoroughness. The works resist the impression of unity and completeness even upon repeated hearings. The consistency in the projection of fragmentary and discontinuous sound clusters does not, however, permit any evocation of playfulness or randomness. To the contrary, it suggests a seriousness that seems all the more immutable through its resistance to our listening. So we are led to assume a rigor that is located outside the sound-event, one that no performance or accumulation of performances can reveal. If we do assume this, then we begin to understand the critical nature of this music: a protest made by its withdrawal from its sound. But we also come to realize that appreciation of this music encompasses two distinct events, neither of which is subsumable to the other. One event is knowing the rule-conditioned properties that specify the score; the other is listening to the performed work.

This distinction—between knowing and listening—provides us with a clearer sense of Adorno's general distinction between traditional and radical music. The service function of traditional music appropriates the score into itself: A score is a professional matter, a part of the procedures through which performances are generated but not in itself a thing for appreciation. Although we may use a score to inform and enhance our listening, the relevant properties are the auditory ones, and the proper subject for appreciation is the performed music. The appreciation that correlates with traditional music identifies enjoyment—however "disinterested"—as its end. As privileged recipient of this end, the listener need not recursively attend to the means as a condition of enjoyment, for the means (i.e., the composing and performing functions) are end-directed. They provide the adequacy of the performed music for the appreciative act.

In the music Adorno champions, however, the relationship between score and performance is not one where the score is subsumable as a means to appreciation; the score, rather, is a subject for appreciation. As such, it shares the appreciative act with the performance. I believe that this dual requirement for the appreciation of radical music underlies Adorno's conception of the dual function of the musical work itself: Such works exemplify formal progress as regards the history of music and project criticism of the society within which the music is composed. In our "decadent" society, the use of traditional music contributes to the illusion that all is well. The satisfactions of harmonic development appropriate to another time are taken—inaccurately—as analogues of the social dynamics of our own time. The enjoyment we find in listening and the self-sufficiency of the concert experience encourage us to apply the same strategies of encapsulation to our dealings with the world. Thus habituated to the equating of appreciation and pleasure, we find the experience of atonal music disconcerting, and we either reject it or mistake it. We reject it if we do not enjoy its sound, and we mistake it if we "manage" to enjoy its sound. In the first case we reject what we hear because it lacks the harmonic predictability to which we are accustomed; in the second case we accept the sound object because we are willing to extend our enjoyment to the apparently chaotic and discontinuous. But in both cases we make our judgments on the basis of listening alone. Adorno remarks that in modern music, where the service function is no longer present, the work is in danger of being taken as an ornament, a mere thing.[17] The paradox here is that appreciation is inadequate whether, in missing the illusion we need, we reject what we hear or, in contenting ourselves with surface, we come to enjoy what we hear.

In atonal music the score exhibits the unconditioned nature of the row. It is unconditioned in the Kantian sense that it is freely taken on but then functions as a binding rule. Fidelity to this rule is a concern that is independent of the concern for the row's exposition through its auditory compliants—the performed sounds. Indeed, the inadequacy of performance in projecting the rule-governed structure of the row serves as a reproach to those who are content to "merely listen." The nonaccessibility of atonal music functions critically in that it identifies the listener's failure to recognize the music's conceptual nature. This failure is seen as a symptom of the more general failure to recognize the nature of society and the need for social transformation.

IV

Adorno construes the dialectic of musical development apocalyptically: He sees it as having stopped, as being frozen in the extremes of its last antithesis—between "gestures of shock" and a "crystalline standstill."[18] In the expressive content of radical music, "passions are no longer simulated, but rather, genuine emotions of the unconscious—of shock, of trauma—are registered without disguise." "Formal ossification" is to be interpreted as the "negation of the severity of life."[19] If we go along with Adorno's claim that music is concerned with "truth," then the truth in radical music is not a pleasant one. About the "general listening public," Adorno remarks, "the dissonances which horrify them testify to their own conditions; for that reason alone do they find them unbearable."[20] The inability to hear the sounds as music makes them unbearable, but then few can identify the form of appreciation that would make them music, and those few already understand the nature of the protest involved. Adorno's polarization of dialectical extremes between "crystal" and "shock" also shows up in his distinction, within radical music, between "expressionist" and "objective" works. In one sense all radical music is expressionist in that its "truth" is obsessed with the ravaged human psyche. In another sense, expressionism represents the last historical stage of incomplete atonality, where vestiges of traditional form strain to preserve the music's accessibility for the general listener and thus render its expressive content both palpable and consequential.[21] In this second sense, objective music is seen as the move away from the thesis of expression into the antithesis of indifference. Adorno says of Schoenberg's late works that they "pose again the question of content regarding subject matter, without pretending to achieve the organic unity of this content with purely musical procedures." Elsewhere he states: "Dissonances arose as the expression of tension, contradiction, and pain. They (now) take on fixed contours and become 'material.' They are no longer the media of subjective expression. For this reason, however, they by no means deny their origin. They become characters of objective protest."[22] But there is a problem here, for I note above that Adorno considered the greatest threat to "new objectivity" to be the possibility of its interpretation as "ornament." How, then, does expression that becomes fixed as "material" retain the power of protest?

How does such acoustic material escape being identified as merely decorative sound and, thus, not consequentially symbolic at all?

The attribution of objectivity to completely atonal works is surely supported by the systematic nature of the twelve-tone row. But if the row is not thoroughly articulate in—cannot be retrieved from—the sound, the listener's volition to include the scored row in appreciation must be located elsewhere. This volition undoubtedly begins with an awareness of the music's context: the social and personal circumstances of its creation. But it proceeds through an incorporation of context into content by relocating these circumstances *in* the work. It concludes by relocating the work itself. As Adorno points out, the typical categories through which we distinguish appreciative capacity (e.g., "layman," "connoisseur," "expert") are of little use here, for these categories are formed within the very institutions against which radical music protests.[23]

The formal intransigence of the row correlates well with the seriousness of the protest. Although use of the row does not preclude sensibility, it is not primarily governed by the appeal to sympathetic distributions of sound. Appreciation in atonal music, then, cannot take as its primary function a progressive sensitivity to the quality of such distributions in performance. I have indicated that the historical development of radical music is marked by failure in social accessibility. If we now define social accessibility as a situating of appreciation in performance, we can hypothesize that musical protest entails using the performance as a referent to something extraneous to it, something nonauditory that nevertheless completes and gives specific identity to the auditory. The imperatives that formed radical music proscribe many characteristics of traditional music. These characteristics are not, as such, irreconcilable with atonality; for example, the row can, in fact, be used to generate harmonic vertical progressions. But the retention of such characteristics—the pursuit of sympathetic sound—produces a contemporary lie: the exaltation of feelings that accord with willful illusion, not actuality.[24] In the expressionist phase of radical music the feelings projected are authentic, but they become increasingly hard to bear; they are progressively fixed at their extremes. Reality is made more painful by the betrayal of hope: the failure of nineteenth-century social ideology in the situations of the twentieth. In his analysis of expressionism, Adorno speaks a good deal of "loneliness"; he also speaks of "impotence." The sexual metaphors here are illuminating: "loneliness" entails a yearning for the contact that brings self-completion; "impotence" entails the inability to assuage loneliness through action. One way of coping with the pain can be found in play, in a retreat to illusion where other identities supplant or replace one's own. But in music Adorno sees this as a corruption of integrity, a historical recidivism that he rejects. Another way out is through a forced indifference to feeling, through an autodissection where feelings lose their interconnectedness in organic subjective experience and are reconstituted in abstract arrays. Here even the desire for accessibility is relinquished, yet for Adorno this constitutes progress: Another historical veil has been pulled aside, and the value of what remains has been affirmed. On this score he states: "expressionism was not sufficiently radical in its position on superstitions regarding the organic. . . . the elimination of the organic resulted in a new crystallization of the concept of the work of art; the works necessarily became heirs to the expressionist heritage."[25]

Traditional music—from which expressionism is not totally emancipated—is characterized by Adorno as "unified" or "hermetic" in structure, which unity, in turn, is based upon the "identity of subject and object." In this regard, Adorno quotes Walter Benjamin's characterization of "hermetic" as "uninterrupted sympathy of the parts with the whole."[26] Objective music, on the other hand, he characterizes as "fragmentary," lacking in unity, and because of this "transformed into protest."[27] In traditional music, the composer's identity—better, intentionality—is transformed into a universalized model in which private individual feelings are replaced by generalized, intersubjectively recognizable "modes" of feeling. This is a way of affirming the thesis that music contains within itself the subjective content of its making and is therefore independent, as regards its meaning, from considerations of the maker or composer. But this thesis, in turn, is based upon the assumption that the musical form presents itself as a basic analogue to the form of subjective experience. Suzanne Langer argues in this way, that the experience of the work is meaningful independently of reference to the experience of its making precisely because it is fundamentally *like* that experience. Of course, the supposition that such an analogue occurs would technically require the posit of an underlying "parent" structure by reference to which the claims of similarity or analogy could be justified. Failing this, one could theorize, as I believe Adorno does, that this thesis of structural commonality between "art and experience"[28] is a historically delimited one which is tenable only so long as neither aspect is found wanting. The "hermetic" nature of art, then, is not music's essential character but only marks a historical stage, one that is now over. As "experience" falls prey to nostalgia and self-deception, "art" relinquishes the formal characteristics that would support the analogue. Radical art thus becomes hostile to traditional art, and "through hostility to art, the work of art approaches knowledge."[29] In radical art, enjoyment is replaced by "perception," specifically, a perception of the music's "lack of unity" and thus—from the traditional standpoint—its "meaninglessness." But a problem arises here: Art that "approaches knowledge" cannot, at the same time, lack meaning.

In traditional music, meaning is found in performance because it is there that music presents itself, ruminates on its own development, and completes itself. Appreciation follows along, and nothing more is needed. In radical music, listening identifies formal fragmentation, a nonhermetic structure that thwarts the sense of completeness. The frustration attendant on searching for the musical work in its performance is what Adorno calls "meaninglessness." This is, perhaps, an infelicitous phrase, but it must be understood in a specific way: the experience of meaninglessness identifies the music's function as protest. The inadequacy of the performed sound of radical music for the needs of an appreciation appropriate to traditional music is not a lack; it is an admonition. It warns against a more serious inadequacy: a perception of the world by the listener such that the traditional forms of meaning would still be wanted and relied upon.

Yet radical music must be rescued as music, for random sound can also properly be experienced as "fragmented." But the meaninglessness of random sound could not maintain the seriousness of protest, that seriousness which forces another interpretation and changes meaninglessness into knowledge. The completeness of radical music is not an arbitrary imposition effected by the listener; it is in the work. It is in that aspect which connects the discontinuous sound fragments to a source that is irreproachably coherent: the row in notation. Although this coherence may not be heard, it can be known, and the inclusion of such knowledge in appreciation gives coherence to the entire work and changes the face of the art.

These days, the designation "modern" is a catalyst for extended rethinking about the nature of historical change in the arts and, correspondingly, about how we define and assess works of art. Our notion of modernity is now "bracketed" and, having lost its role as designator of present practices, has become identified with values of a period in the historical past. My discussion here has largely been about one concern that is characteristic of this period: artistic form and social theory joined under the linked concepts of progress and protest. Interpreting Adorno, I have proposed that we construe certain artworks as entities which join theoretic and physical aspects in their ontology.[30] In his context of radical music, such artworks function as social instruments as well as formal exemplars. The postscript that suggests itself is the question as to how Adorno's particular thesis has fared over time: the time of transition into the period sometimes identified as late modernism or, later, as postmodernism. Does "Adorno–Schoenberg" remain an adequate doctrinal support for a music whose ambition, after all, is to persevere in its claim of greatness? Or, conversely, does Schoenberg need "rescuing" from Adorno's "failed" sociology? Only a few comments are possible here: We cannot suppose that Schoenberg "rid of" Adorno is Schoenberg "plain," only Schoenberg rethought. If it is the case, as I have suggested above, that interpretations may be counted as proper parts of artworks, then it should follow that we can assess them aesthetically. Under this assumption Adorno has a chance: At the least, his thesis has intensity, scope, elegance, and, importantly, goes beyond the values of "mere" (Adorno would say "bourgeois") sensibility. To be sure, we cannot stay with Adorno; he is too pointed, too preoccupied with old wounds. But he conceives of art as crucial in a way that we will be hard put to match.

"Appreciation," "Obligation," and an Artwork's End

My general concern in this chapter is with limits upon the status of artwork and particularly with the question as to whether and how such status, once properly attained, may be lost. In the history of philosophic thought, the emergence of aesthetics as a distinct area of inquiry with its own special concerns is relatively recent. Yet in a certain sense this victory, however hard-won, may have become too complete. The aesthetic, from the standpoint of its autonomy, can be radically interpreted as a license to stand aloof from other ways in which objects and events are understood and evaluated. Such "aestheticizing" of the world becomes problematic when, in the light of these other, nonaesthetic, experiences, we ask if everything in the world merits aesthetic identity or, conversely, whether we are ever justified in engaging any and all things from an aesthetic point of view. Additionally, we may ask how our answers to these questions affect our appreciation of art. We usually consider artworks to be a special kind of aesthetic object, but this is not self-evident. Problems of the above kind arise not only when we are uncertain about the limits of the aesthetic but also when we come to wonder whether artworks need be included in it.

There are things in the world that are artworks and others that are not. Some things in the world we appreciate, and to others we are obligated in certain ways. These two sets of descriptions, when brought together, generate interesting questions. Certainly, of the things we appreciate, some but not all are artworks. But, among the many things we do not appreciate, are there any that we may not—are obligated not to—appreciate? Then, too, we need not appreciate all artworks. But, among the things that are art, are there any—better, ought there be any—of the kind that we may not appreciate? "Appreciation" and "obligation" are both "value" terms, and they usually occur in different realms of value theory, the first in aesthetics and the second in ethics. My concern, here, is about a situation in which these realms overlap, about circumstances where the applicability of both types of terms seems justified. Such circumstances identify the issue that titles this chapter: the "end" of artworks. I suggest in a preliminary way that eventualities of this kind may occur when an act of appreciation comes into conflict with a prescribed obligation.

By an artwork's end I do not mean anything like the end of a "performance," or a "reading," or even a "looking," for I am interested here in the status of the extended work, not in the fortunes of its instances. I hold that "being art" is not a natural kind of being, like being human; it is rather a conventional kind, like being a citizen. As a human, I can become inhuman but not nonhuman. My status as a citizen, however, is vulnerable in the case that I do not—or am seen not to—comply with the rules that govern citizenship. I suggest that artworks are similarly vulnerable, that there are a number of ways in which their status as art may be lost to them.

In this chapter I propose to examine one of the several conditions that I believe affect the status of artwork.[1] I raise the question as to how a conflict of "accounts" or "interpretations" of some event may cause the loss of such status. The examples I provide for my main argument are from the performing arts, but I develop my case somewhat indirectly. I first consider whether the more inclusive realm of aesthetic entities is bounded by any constraints—whether there are things that ought not be appreciated—and I develop a distinction between "appreciation" and "appreciability" through the concept of approval. I approach "nonappreciability" through the concept of obligation, and I suggest that certain forms of obligation are incompatible not only with aesthetic appreciation but also with the status of artwork. I then consider a situation in which something nonappreciable is nevertheless proposed as an artwork and the proposal is then challenged. The disagreement here is caused not by a conflict in taste but, rather, by a conflict between the exercise of taste and the fulfillment of an obligation. Finally, I show that an artwork may first be acknowledged and then rejected as art when (1) a clear priority between accounts does exist and (2) the artwork is reinterpreted through a subsequent account that includes within it an art-defeating obligation.

II

First, I must lay some preparatory groundwork by examining the four interrelated concepts *appreciation, approval, appreciability,* and *obligation.* We usually distinguish between "appreciating" and "approving of" when "approving" is taken in its ethical sense. Thus, for example, we need not appreciate what we approve of, although we usually approve of the things we appreciate. There are times, however, when we want to stretch our sophistication, and so we test our ability to appreciate things that are somewhat shocking or ordinarily distasteful. But few of us would apply this test to the realm of things or events we unequivocally find to be loathsome or that we condemn. There are, in fact, some things that none of us would appreciate, but, of course, this depends on how one defines "us." It could be argued that the very notion of appreciation depends upon some codification of "us" from which we then derive the differentia between the things we allow or disallow.

It is also useful to distinguish between "appreciation" and "appreciability": We appreciate only what we find appreciable, although we need not appreciate everything we find appreciable. The parallel with "approval" suggests itself, but it is not a complete one. Approval admits of great variety and almost infinite degree, whereas appreciability seems to be binary in structure. We need to reach some substantial strength of disapproval before we consider something to be nonappreciable. The modality of this determination is, of course, one of "ought not" rather than "cannot," that is, an imperative holding for a certain construal of "us," identified in part by what we reasonably expect of one another in such matters.

If something is appreciable, we are free to account for it aesthetically; we can—although we need not—appreciate it. Accordingly, we predicate "non-appreciability" of a thing or event when its aesthetic account is *precluded* by the greater force of some other, nonaesthetic, account. This preclusion is causally related to another account of the thing in question, one that indicates that we ought—in the strong sense of "are obligated"—to respond to that thing in a way other than appreciation. In this context, the other account identifies a certain action or set of actions as necessary or strongly desirable. Furthermore, it indicates that the obligation to perform such actions would be thwarted or weakened by the act of appreciating that thing or event. I suggest that, in general, accounts of different kinds stand to each other in inhibitory as well as enabling relationships. Such accounts as may inhibit the aesthetic derive from interests or needs that have greater *urgency* in our scale of values than does the aesthetic.

In this regard, let us consider the role of the "connoisseur." One who is said to have "advanced" or "exquisite" taste carries more of a burden than the rest of us who merely show "good" taste; the higher reaches of taste require creativity in addition to simple diligence. Thus, connoisseurs are often drawn to unlikely subjects, to things that are vaguely repulsive, disconcerting, or unwholesomely attractive. Although too adventurous connoisseurs risk being run out of town, their reward—if they are careful—is first a collective incredulity, then agreement, and, eventually, acclaim. Note that this process does not move neutral or indifferent things toward appreciation; rather, it offers things that, antecedently, were clearly regarded as inappropriate but, in retrospect, not sufficiently so as to deny their new aesthetic identity.

What is or is not aesthetically appreciable is a matter of what something exemplifies—a matter of the qualities it shares with certain other things. To suggest an unlikely candidate for aesthetic appreciation is also to attempt to aesthetically redeem a part of the world, the part that stands in a similarity relationship with that candidate. Such an attempt may be as innocuous as promoting a taste for brandied bumblebees or as charged as attributing "redeeming features" to a particular "depravity" in order to rescue it from prohibition. An artwork, however, has a more complex structure than do "merely" aesthetic objects. With artworks the question arises as to what may properly be designated—depicted or described—within the limitations of the category "art."

When artworks function didactically, as evidently some do, they are less pervious to the vagaries and limits of appreciability. Consequently, they may safely be concerned with the grimmer aspects of theological, political, or ethical subjects. The proper elucidation of such subjects depends at least as much upon exhibiting what is reprehensible as upon affirming the desirable. The sensuous characteristics of artworks make them well suited for this task, perhaps because the sensuous and the reprehensible have an old tradition of linkage. Images of hell are more evocative and easier to get at than images of heaven. The history of art is replete with martyrdoms, massacres, and other horrors or, more precisely, images of horror. So if I ask whether there are subjects that cannot be imaged in artworks, the answer seems to be no. Certain *things* may indeed be beyond the pale of aesthetic appreciability, but their *images* are not outside the scope of art. Thus, it seems that art protects us from the demands that things would make were we to meet them as neither images nor artworks.

But, as we know, distinctions between images and things are not always clear. If it is true, therefore, that some things are such that we approve of their images but not of them, we should want to be sure that we can make the distinction. Actually, this difficulty may occur in the realms of both aesthetic things and artworks. Certain things may be horrifying or intolerable from one vantage point and not from another. This conflict in interpretations might be understood as simply a need for further clarification, or it could indicate a lack of cohesion in the community proper—a competition between different construals of "us." Similarly, we attempt to differentiate between the characteristics of images that artworks project and characteristics of other images that are produced for nonartistic reasons. But to what extent, if at all, does our knowledge of such "extraneous" data affect our interpretation of what we "see"—whether or when we consider it art? I now offer some examples that purport to illustrate these concerns. I begin with one that questions the *limits of appreciability*, continue with another that considers tensions between *aesthetic* and *artistic*, and conclude with a third that tests the distinctions between *images* and *things imaged*.

III

Let us suppose that you and I are standing on a highway overpass watching traffic speed by. Suddenly a car careens across the median strip and smashes into another head on. What is your response? I suspect that, whatever else it may be, it would not include aesthetic pleasure. But why exactly? Certainly there is much in the event that is "vivid" and "dramatic," even "richly textured" and "unified." These are all, in the abstract, often counted as aesthetic properties. Why not now? One answer might be that your sense of horror and compassion "precludes," "leaves no room for," "is antithetical to" an aesthetic response. Yet you might respond similarly to a skillful film depiction of such an event but with the difference that your response would then include an awareness of aesthetic qualities, and the depth and dimension of your feelings would correlate in some measure with the richness of these qualities. What precludes this sort of correlation in the actual event? The reason, I suggest, is that the interpretation called for there includes an obligation to do something—to attempt to better the situation in any way possible. This seems to follow from a prior obligation to have kept the cars from crashing had you been able to do so. Even if you actually could not have helped on either count and thus, via the "ought implies can" dictum, escape actual obligation, certainly this does not give you reason to construe the event aesthetically.

I am offering this argument not as an ethical rule but rather as a description of what I take to be the response that "you" and "I"—"all of us"— would have in such circumstances. "Us," as I state above, indicates common membership in a community where we would expect "everyone" to react generally as we do. The pervasiveness of this expectation is, in fact, one of the demarcators of this community.

Having said this, I now complicate matters a bit. Let us further imagine a third person, a stranger, who watches the crash with us and who exclaims, with evident glee, "Wasn't that beautiful!" How can we account for this response? Two possibilities suggest themselves: (1) The individual is an alien who did not know that people were involved or, more extremely, knew and did not care; (2) the individual is not an alien but a psychopath. In the case of the alien, if he indeed mistook the incident as, say, that of a malfunction in an automated system, then we could suppose that more complete information would bring forth a more appropriate response—more like "ours"—and would thereby identify the alien, in this regard at least, as being "one of us." If, on the other hand, he knew that people were involved and did not care, then we would require some "mapping" of the alien community's value system to understand the disjunction between his response and ours. We might find here that some pattern of constraints between accounts occurs in his system as well, although they might not be acceptable or completely intelligible to us. However, if the inappropriate response is that of a psychopath, then we purportedly have someone who is a member of our community but, for whatever traumatic reasons, misjudges and misuses the available symbolic structures. When we wish to discover some pattern of constraints on the aesthetic by following this analysis, however, we meet with some difficulties.

Appreciation, as we know, has to do with the exercise of taste. But aberrations in taste, as I have pointed out, are the province not only of the psychopath but also of the connoisseur (assuming here that they are mutually exclusive). Mere "bad taste" is usually not associated with either, for its exercise is comfortably moderate, trivial in particulars, and not the sort of thing that threatens to displace obligations. But "aberrant" or "advanced" taste is more extreme and need not be trivial in either its experience or its consequences, for it invariably identifies a novel and untested realm for its subject. In the long run, whether such extreme responses are rejected as madness or hailed as aesthetic liberation is a matter of whether the members of a given community are willing to redefine certain of their other beliefs in order to sustain the inclusion of heretofore "taboo" subjects within the aesthetic.

Still, the act of appreciation is essentially a private one, for it is first manifested in a "feeling" which, to be "had," requires no intersubjective agreement or public manifestation. So it is not until the third spectator *expresses* his pleasure at the sight of the crash that we react by asserting that he ought not appreciate such things. Note, however, that we do not mean by this that the individual could have *decided* not to appreciate the crash, nor do we mean that a necessary component of his appreciation is its expression. It is important to *our* understanding of the third spectator's experience that we hear him exclaim, "Isn't that beautiful!" But his—as we judge it, misplaced—appreciation of the event required no overt indication on his part. If he said nothing and did not help in the rescue, we would only criticize his failure to act upon an evident obligation. If he manifested his enjoyment, we would deplore his deviant capacity but not expect his help. If he kept silent and did help us, not because of a perceived obligation but perhaps because of a peripheral sensitivity to clues of appropriate behavior, we, knowing nothing further, would be satisfied. But, then, so would he.

IV

Now, I move my concerns from the realm of the aesthetic to that of art. The example I use in this section presents a situation that is comparable in its negative qualities to the one just discussed. This time, however, there is agreement among all concerned that the event is *not* appreciable. The disagreement occurs, rather, over the issue as to whether an obligation to interfere in the event can properly be put aside *in the case that the event is construed as a work of art.* Here we are faced not with the question of a deviant capacity but with a conflicting theory, one that denies that our obligations to interfere are most appropriate to the situation. We might consider this theory also to be deviant. But how do we show this, particularly if the theory attracts a number of supporters—a different "community"?

I offer the following: A person, antecedently established as an artist, presents a "new work." He undertakes a series of tableaux in a public art gallery that consist of acts of self-mutilation. These acts are not theatrical illusions but are actual inflictions. As a consequence the artist dies. If we were to take that individual in isolation, as we do the third spectator in our last example, we could also regard these acts as psychopathological and feel justified in attempting to stop them. Yet in this case, let us suppose, we encounter a whole apparatus of the "artworld": spectators, critics, gallery officials, and so on, who, rather than attempting to interfere with the artist's actions, engage in the critical and promotional activity typically associated with art exhibitions—activities of the kind we ordinarily take to be confirmatory for the status "art."

The claim, then, that those actions constitute an artwork extends beyond the solitary individual, about whom we might argue that he was not (then) functioning as an artist, and moves into a collective context. We now encounter a consensual group affirming the bizarre incidents as art, and we are faced with a certain fait accompli, a *transaction*, in which the triad of artist-work-spectator has been formed that has characteristics similar to those in other transactions where we find that "art" occurs. From this similarity comes confirmatory strength for the claim of art and for the authenticity of the identities of the participants.

Nevertheless, let us suppose that we reject the claim and insist that the incident is a case of madness and the rest a horrible sham. To counter our position, arguments could be offered that are at least intelligible, if not acceptable, to us. The other group might freely admit, for example, that the incidents in question *are* bizarre and, within a certain framework, pathological. But a different basis for the function of art might be offered. For example, decrying the "decadent formalism" of our day, the individuals involved might regard themselves as setting about to "revitalize" art by basing it upon, say, a religious notion of transcendence through self-immolation, or upon a political notion of social protest through personal expiation, or some other similar rationale.

Of course, we might, unphilosophically, reject such arguments out of hand, and, if our own views were sufficiently reinforced by legal statutes, we could have prohibitions imposed. This recourse would open up another issue for discussion, namely, the social censorship of artworks and whether such actions are ever justified. But this is a complex topic which I cannot pursue here. So, for present purposes, our only recourse is to present arguments against construing that incident as art. We might begin by admitting that actions such as self-mutilation could be justified within certain extraordinary circumstances. But we would maintain that such actions can be understood as ethical or political responses, not as artworks. To conflate the two, we would insist, is to weaken and perhaps deny the authenticity of either. Additionally, we might point out that such incidents, if accepted as art, could quickly lose their didactic overlay and perhaps come to be *enjoyed* in ways that we enjoy *aesthetic* objects. This outcome, presumably, neither side would want.

Such arguments might or might not prevail. If our arguments were accepted, then the groups in conflict would join together in a single context. From the standpoint of this context a category mistake was made and later recognized. The incident in question, then, was not an artwork, although for a time it (mistakenly) was thought to be one. The question of an artwork's "end," therefore, does not apply here. Let us suppose, on the other hand, that our arguments do not prevail. We then have a conflict between theories.

If the members of both sides perceive the reasons given in support of each argument as intelligible—although from each separate vantage point as unconvincing—then we might all regard the theories as incompatible yet entertain hope that further discussion will bring about resolution. But, however this is decided, our central concern is still unaddressed. For, under our account, the incident *never was* art or, conversely, if we are persuaded otherwise, *still is* art. More pessimistically, if both sides regard the conflicting theories as incommensurable,[2] as lacking common linguistic criteria for the application of such terms as "art," then the question becomes moot. In this case, my thesis is still not demonstrated, but now for the reason that the realm to which it applies is not discriminable. Here we might well have arrived at the Hegelian prediction come true: "The end of art." But I only want to show how "an artwork ends." So let me try a last approach.

V

In the preceding section I raise the question as to whether something that is not appreciable—that should not be enjoyed—can be an artwork. I conclude there that any cogent answer to this question requires agreement as to the conditions of applicability of the term "art." If there is not agreement, then, as indicated above, *that* problem must be faced before the other discussion proceeds. On the other hand, if there is agreement, if we "all" agree, for example, that unappreciable things should not be art, then we might only want to say that any attribution to the contrary constitutes a *mistake*. Unfortunately, this does not demonstrate my thesis that an artwork can end, for a mistaken attribution only shows that the thing in question has never achieved that status, not that it has lost it.

It is difficult to argue against another's proposal that some particular thing is art because, in one well-known sense, the proposal constitutes that thing *as* art.[3] Accordingly, for me to deny that something is art seems to fail just when another affirms it. But this seeming catholicity in the attributive act is deceptive, for it depends, as I believe, upon the *innocuousness* of what is considered for art status, even though this dependency masquerades as a principle of nonexclusion. For example, when some ordinary blocks of ice were presented as sculpture in a recent exhibition,[4] the presentation evoked the by now familiar fuss; there were those who were outraged and others who were delighted. But nothing much else really seemed at stake, for the ice, were it *not* considered an artwork, would have done nothing more in the museum where it lay than what it did do: It melted and created a puddle. We may be so accustomed, these days, to think of the realm of art as embracing all the world that we fail to see that our openness to "new" prospects is an openness largely to things that do not much matter—in ways other than as artworks. But my concerns here are with things that are, or are presumed to be, art and that *do* matter in other ways, ways that compete with the aesthetic in accounting for these things.

My focus in this section is on the possibility that one resolution of this "competition" between accounts can result in an artwork's end. The question to be answered is whether we can *properly* experience something as art that we subsequently learn is the sort of thing that *should not* be art. "Properly," here, indicates the distinction between a mistaken attribution and an actual loss of status. What this distinction comes to is taken up in the course of the discussion.

Now I proceed to my last example and ask that we imagine the following: We are invited to a showing of new works by some experimental filmmakers. Among the notable films of the evening is one that employs a collage technique in which footage exhibiting different styles, and ostensibly from different sources, is spliced together. The episodes that constitute the film are related thematically, and the success of the film hangs upon the thematic exposition's acting to unify what is otherwise perceived as a somewhat disjointed sequence. The theme in question has to do with aspects of life in decaying urban environments, and a number of episodes are quite violent. At this time, I remain unconvinced about the overall success of this particular film, but I am impressed by a number of its qualities: the contrasts between allusion and stark realism, the complexity of the metaphors, and the sheer pictorial force of some parts. Seeing the film as a whole requires that I expend a good deal of effort synthesizing the disparate imagery, but I feel that acceding to this somewhat unusual demand has increased my appreciation of the film and my understanding of the medium. Further, I find that the brutality of some episodes is effectively "distanced" by the film's apparently discontinuous structure, and I include the dislocations themselves in the film's fictional world.

Later in the evening, after all the films have been shown, their makers engage in a discussion of the various efforts. We are then told about this particular film that only parts of it are professionally made, that other parts comprise documentary footage of various kinds, including one episode that is a gangland filming of a murder as it is being committed—a "snuff" film. I now realize that my previous reactions to the film are being compromised in a number of ways by this new information: I am now uncomfortable with my memories of "appreciating"—particularly with my synthesizing efforts on behalf of the film's continuity. I do recollect the murder episode as a short and not especially notable one, but I now strive to bring it back in every detail, and I find that my urgency here is acting to suppress my memory of the film's other episodes. On another count, I feel some anger at what I take to be the filmmaker's deceit, for I see that he has tricked us into misconceiving a constitutive aspect of the film, the one having to do with its "origins of production."[5] This deceit—as I now begin to believe—affects not only the artistic value of the film but its very status as an artwork.

So I proceed to challenge both the film and its maker. I argue that the film is now *compromised* as art, for it can no longer be seen as a unity or "whole." The new information about the source of the one episode tells me that the *intention* behind its filming is compatible with the intention to commit murder. As I find murders and their acquiescent filmings both to be unappreciable, I hold that the film is not (now) art. I argue further that, although the filmmaker evidently took pains not to reveal the origins of that problematic episode either within the film or within the context of its showing, he did include the probability of our *misconceiving* these origins within the context of its showing. On this count, I accuse the filmmaker of *not intending* to make an artwork but, rather, of engaging in a demonstration of power—a manipulation of his audience.

However, as is the case with experimental film showings, counterarguments are usually forthcoming. The maker of the film reminds us that documentary footage is often used for fictional purposes and that, in any case, questions about sources are questions about nonconstitutive, nonvisual properties that are irrelevant to the film's status as art and also should be irrelevant to its appreciation—although they might bear on its identity as a social document. The filmmaker also reminds me of my own earlier remarks to the effect that, as far as paintings are concerned, there seem to be no constraints upon what may be imaged or depicted. Inasmuch as films, he contends, are also composed of images and illusions, my argument—that certain things are unappreciable because they call for other kinds of actions—also does not hold for film. Film images, he states, are like painted images in the respect that, artistically, they refer only to the action within the film, and therefore our only requisite reaction is the one we would perform in imagination. Regarding my claim that he did not "intend" to make art, the filmmaker replies that intentions in art are even less relevant than sources: They are exceedingly difficult to ascertain, and even if, in a given instance, they could be ascertained adequately, the causal argument from "intention" to "work," as we all know, is notoriously weak.[6]

These are strong if familiar arguments and, in answering them, I must be careful to keep clear the principal points I want to make. I do not deny that, upon seeing the film, I appreciated it as an artwork, but I maintain that I do not now. However, I also want to argue that I did not make a "mistake" when I appreciated the film, and I continue to affirm that *that* film is art. But what I do not appreciate now is not the film I first saw but the film I asked to see for a second time, after the discussion about its origins. During this second showing I find that I pay attention primarily to the filmed murder, the rest having come to seem both trivial and incidental. I experience no desire now to view the film as a whole—to integrate that episode with the others— for I want to see how the episode is, not how it fits.

Although I recognize the morbid taint in the singleness of my attention, I take this not as a weakness in my appreciative capabilities but rather as an unadmirable residue of my sense of helplessness. The murder, after all, is a crime, an act that should require a particular social response. I suggest here, as I did in the first example—that of the car crash—that appreciation is not among the appropriate responses. The filming of the murder may give it a premeditated cast but does not change its characteristics into aesthetic ones. Correspondingly, my knowing the nature of the film but having no recourse to action does not license me then to accept it as an artwork. As I view it the second time, the film is not an aesthetic whole, for parts of it have a stronger correlation with things outside the film than they do with its other parts. Thus, at the second showing, I insist that the film fails as art.

The filmmaker's argument to the point that both painterly and film images have an essential fictionality about them—that despite knowledge of sources and intentions they cannot be seen explicitly to denote—also seems flawed to me. I agree that, however detailed and "realistic" a painted depiction may be, we are never sure that what is represented is anything other than a product of the imagination. But in film it seems to be the other way around. Despite all fictional trappings and effects, we can never be sure that what we see is not actual, in the sense that a filmed representation also denotes a reality that is independent of the fictional world of the film. Of course, the fact that our information about a work is incomplete need not compromise it artistically, for we never do have complete information about any work, and though learning more usually changes our interpretation it seldom threatens the status of the work. Yet I also maintain that there are things we can learn that will lead us to see an artwork as something other than art. I argue that the exampled film is compromised as art by the single aberrant episode, and I note here that my argument includes, as a contributing factor, the film-maker's intentions.[7]

In this regard, let us further suppose that the filmmaker knows about the source of the episode and admits that he meant to deceive us. But, after my arguments, he attempts to justify his actions in still another way: "My *real* intention," he states, "is not simply to deceive you but to make an artwork that *includes* you and your reactions to the new information; my complete work is actually a theater piece with the film as one part and you and your reactions as another; the deceit, therefore, is a necessary structural element of this work." My reply is that, although his intentions might possibly be rescued as "art-affirming" on this score, he has, in fact, shown us what might be another constraint on art: that an artwork should not include persons who are *unwilling* to be—who have no intention of being—part of it. But I have no time to further this argument. Finally, let us suppose that a third party informs us that it is he who actually filmed the murder, that his intentions were to make an artwork, and that he enjoyed himself enormously. In reply—from a safe distance—I deny that his intentions, explicit as they are, countermand the other characteristics that defeat the film as art. I suggest here that *both* his actions and his intentions are inappropriate in much the same way as were those of the psychopath in my first example.

VI

What is there now to say about my thesis of an artwork's end? Perhaps the following: Through this example I suggest a situation in which a film is an artwork when first seen and ceases to be an artwork upon second showing. I take "what I saw" and "what I knew" at that first time to provide *sufficient* indicators, although not necessary ones, for the film's status as art. These indicators also led me to appreciate the film in certain ways. The second time around, a new indicator emerges, of the kind that does not simply alter the quality of my appreciation but generates an account of the film that turns out to be incompatible with its status as art. But now we may ask why this change cannot be explained as a mistake on my part, one that is later rectified. After all, I argue in the previous example that upholding that event as art constitutes a mistake. But I think there is a crucial difference between the two situations, and this difference has to do with the adequacy of a theory relative to the situation it purports to account for.

In section III I hold that the theory which takes the mutilation as art is inadequate relative to other ways the event is also understood at that time. If within this—assumedly unified—context of occurrence such accounts as "———— is art" and "———— is unappreciable" are accepted as being incompatible, then the latter excludes the former. In the present case, however, the film is first seen at a time when all other accounts, given the available information, are compatible with its status as an artwork. Further, the information then available is adequate within the conventional range of expectations about what needs to be known in such cases. Taking the film as art, therefore, seems to me to be a bona fide instance of a proper attribution and not a mistake. However, at a later time, when new information generates an account of the film that excludes its status as art, then any attribution to the contrary at *that* time *is* a mistake.

This correlation between the temporal factor and status change is important here. For instance, if we were to insist that *all* present status is contingent upon future interpretations, then we would deny ourselves the possibility of accepting *anything* as art, except in the tentative way that compromises the fullness of the experience. In general, a film, construed as art, corresponds with *some* class of instances of its showings. As regards the film here in question, the class of showings is finite and its members denumerable. We know how many showings that film *as art* has, for we know that its last performance occurred just prior to our learning about the source of the one episode. Any subsequent showings of the film, therefore, are of it as something *other* than art. This seems to constitute a bona fide instance of an artwork's end.

VII

In summary, my thesis here is about a particular correlation between the realms of aesthetics and ethics. The entities that I describe as nonappreciables are such that the situations they generate require the response of remedial or compensatory action. This requirement is in the nature of an ethical obligation to interfere in the situation at hand with the intention of "bettering" it as the case may require. In some situations no action is possible, but the obligation persists through our belief that the desirability of a situation of that kind where action would be possible is greater than the one that actually obtains. I argue that the recognition of such an obligation amounts to an interpretation of a thing or event within which an ethical response takes precedence over, and *precludes*, an aesthetic response. There is no assurance, however, that any such interpretation will continue to maintain its dominant position, just as no artwork is assured of the continuance of its status as art. It may be that beyond certain limits of time and culture there are no nonappreciables, but these limits, too, are not constant.

I do not agree with the formalist thesis that art is only about art. For, if this were really so, then the only proper response to a work would be appreciation. But I believe this often to be a partial and inadequate response. These days too little attention is paid to experiences of art that go beyond, or do not include, appreciation. I am concerned with this possibility here. Although there is some present interest in the cognitive or conceptual aspects of art, the ethical dimension has fared less well. This is due, perhaps, to the history of unfortunate couplings of works and dogmas, from Savonarola through totalitarian art. My thesis, however, is not about what works should or should not propose—they can propose anything or nothing—nor is it about what works should be; it is, rather, about what works should not be. I suggest that there are works whose functions extend beyond appreciation in that they test the strengths of our moral prohibitions, and I argue that such works are ontically vulnerable. In the ensuing conflict between accounts, a defeat for the work may result not only in its devaluation but in its *end* as a work. A prohibited entity, in this regard, is not art because consideration of its aesthetic characteristics is blocked by held ethical beliefs. Under certain circumstances, a once appropriate aesthetic interpretation can be *withdrawn* via reinterpretation and thereby cause the entity to end as an artwork.

If we agree that art is a concept that identifies a compatibility relationship between certain things we make and uses we make of them, then it is not surprising that we find some things that do not fit and some uses that are inappropriate. It should also not be surprising, inasmuch as we group things for other reasons as well, that these "compatibility circles" influence and modify each other on an ongoing basis. What is surprising is that artworks are often considered to be exempt from this process: We may agree that they have conventional beginnings, but for some of us their durations quickly become "transcendent" and, although open to changes in value, become immune to changes in status.[8] This is a permanence that we would not admit either for our theories about the physical world or for our precepts of ethical behavior. Yet it remains one of the (to my mind, expendable) dogmas about artworks. There are all sorts of interesting theoretical and venal reasons for this; I have considered some of them here and look at others in the chapter that follows.

Artworks that End
and Objects that Endure

My inquiry, in the preceding chapters, into the status designated by the term "artwork" serves to emphasize the ontological volatility of this status. The focus of recent discussions of this question has been largely on "beginnings," that is, how things come to be art and what bearing, if any, determinate aesthetic "qualities" or "attitudes" have on the attributive act. There has been little said, however, about endings, about whether the status of artwork, once achieved, is as durable as ordinary usage indicates and, if not, under what conditions such status can be lost. In this chapter I pay some attention to beginnings, but primarily as a pathway to a further consideration of endings. My general orientation in these matters is a contextualist one, for I believe that the determination of something as an artwork does not depend upon any special properties that all and only artworks purportedly hold in common. My view is that, given such constraints as those I describe in chapter 4, artworks can be many sorts of things although the sort that each is becomes special—and constitutive of the class—as a *consequence* of that thing's having become art. I do not deny that the artworks we know are all special in certain ways, and hence distinguishable as art, but I contend that what is special about them gives us little help in locating some things that are novel works.

A contextualist theory of beginnings typically replaces the requirement of matching between novel and extant works with other types of requirements. Some of these may focus upon the mode of selection, as in Dickie's "candidate-agent" thesis;[1] others may stress the arena of selection, as in Danto's thesis of the "artworld."[2] It would seem reasonable that a compatible theory of endings should also avoid criteria based upon norms or paradigms and, instead, focus upon performative acts and their enabling theories. But the wanted parallelism cannot be completely sustained, for the loss of art status has its own special requirements. To show this let us assume agreement with Dickie's thesis that under conditions of "artifactuality" and "candidacy," anything can be art.[3] We might then assume that any such thing could become a candidate for status loss and, in like manner, *cease* being art. But here the parallelism breaks down. For if Dickie is right that a single "agent-of-the-artworld" can confer status, then it should follow that for something already art the continued affirmation of only one such agent is required to *sustain* it as art. So it is evident that an artwork's end cannot occur through a single defeating performative, or even by "popular demand." Something stronger is required, and I have described this requirement in chapter 4. Briefly, it is this: The status of artwork can be lost through the demonstration of some incompatibility between the continuation of such status and the application of another—more proper or urgent—interpretation of the object in question. My earlier discussion concerned incompatibilities between aesthetic and ethical accounts of a thing or event. Here, I explore another way in which an artwork might "cease being art."

In this chapter I again concentrate on the visual arts because formulation of the problem of status attainment and durability is particularly critical for this realm. The works I use as examples for my discussion can be interpreted as those that "are," or "contain," epistemic riddles: works that incorporate doubt about their identity as art into their subject matter. What these works seem to be about, in other words, *includes* whether they are—or can be found out to be—artworks. These observations apply not only to the many works in the direct traditions of Duchamp and dada but also to more recent and less guileful pieces, variously characterized as earthworks, performance pieces, conceptual works, and so on, which also elude the standard categories that we use to sort out visual works. One—by this time familiar—eluding stratagem can be found in a work masquerading as an ordinary object in the world. Duchamp's urinal piece, or *Fountain*, is an early paradigm of this type. Although we may not be sure *that* it is an artwork or, less severely, *why* it is an artwork, we are hard-pressed to find defeating conditions that do not also endanger other things we want to keep as art. Yet, by the same token, we have equal difficulty here in finding enabling conditions that *affirm* the work's status as art but do not also let in other things we want to exclude.

Such difficulties do not linger on indefinitely, however. *Fountain* is now undeniably art, and its early provocations only serve to teach us how to include our uncertainty about a thing's identity within our appreciations. One might suppose, given such a lesson, that we would come to expect some uncertainties about the duration of artworks. Might we not now want to include in our appreciation of some work the anticipation that it could *cease* being art?

Another reason why certain questions of status attainment and loss are particularly relevant to the visual arts comes from the formal nature of such works: from the criteria through which we typically sort out artworks according to sense realm and symbol-type. Among philosophers who generally agree that artworks are not identical with physical objects, there remains controversy about what else they might be. In the literature, artworks have been identified, variously, as classes, types, kinds, individuals, and so on. Disagreement also persists, given the panoply of available symbol-parts, over the exact location of the "work" in each of the art forms, whether it is to be equated with a score, or performance, or text, or reading, and so on. I cannot take up these issues here, but my present thesis does not depend upon some particular construal of artwork or location of its ontological status. However one decides to do this, the question of a work's end still presents special problems for the visual arts.

In this regard let us look at our experiences of the individual arts and compare the patterns that mark the appreciative act in each of them. We ordinarily think of musical works as ending, in the sense that their performances occur within specific delimited time spans. Such spans, despite variations in interpretation, we find to be consistent enough between different performances of a work to reinforce our counting these performances as instances of the same work. Books do not "end themselves" in this way; it is we who "finish them." Nevertheless, books, like plays and symphonies, *do* have ends although, with books, each of us takes his individual time about getting there. Paintings and sculptures, however, seem not to be like that. Of course we may look and look again; and I suppose we sometimes say that we have "looked enough." But the works have no ends that might correspond to the end of our attention. Concerning music: I may walk away from a performance, but to do so constitutes a value judgment, about the music or my own capacities; more usually I remain until the performance ends, until the auditory object is no more. When I have once read a book and walked away, the book remains. Yet, even here, in having read that book I perforce have followed the sequence of its language—word upon sentence upon paragraph—and, whatever my digressions and lapses, I have read the book the same way as we all do: to its end. When I look at a painting and then walk away, the painting, like a book, remains. Yet, however long I look at it my attention is end-directed only in regard to my experience but not in regard to what comprises that painting. In his "notational analysis," Goodman points out that, syntactically, there are no "characters" in paintings that the painted marks are "inscriptions" of, or—what comes to the same thing—the marks that compose a painting are in a "dense" array.[4] Thus, there is no quantifiable aggregate of inscriptions that we can "get through." Much has been said about proper ways to "read" paintings, but what is proposed are conventions of style, not language, for no way can show when any such reading would be complete.

II

I suggest that a painting does not end at a particular time as does a performance, nor can it be read to its end as one does a book. It is neither an event nor a linguistic entity but rather is an obdurate object of immediate perception whose identity seems inextricably wedded to its duration as an object. But, if this is so, how then can such a work end short of its physical destruction? Evidently, as I hold that this does occur, I must reject the thesis of work-object identity for artworks. I introduce my position by referring to Joseph Margolis's concept of "embodiment."[5] Margolis argues that artworks are "culturally emergent" entities and, as such, are distinguishable from the physical objects or events through which they are made manifest. Works are construed as being embodied in rather than as identical with their physical counterparts; both these aspects are identified as particulars, thus avoiding ontic commitment to universals. The paired entities relate to each other in certain specified ways: An occurrence of the embodied work presupposes the existence of its embodying object; the work possesses, indeed must possess, certain properties—"functional or intentional properties"—that its paired object does not possess. These specifications are supported by a distinction made by Jack Glickman in a discussion on creativity that Margolis here incorporates.[6] Glickman distinguishes between "made" and "created" entities and in this way accounts for the ontic change when, for example, a "made" artifact such as a urinal is later "created" by Duchamp as the "urinal piece," an artwork. Also, contra Dickie,[7] Glickman argues that a so-called natural object, a piece of driftwood, say, may remain untouched and still be "created" as art. Artifacture, on this account—unlike Dickie's— is not a necessary condition for the status of art. "Creating" is identified here as the status-endowing function, but its exercise does not always entail physically changing those things to which it applies.

These distinctions can be useful for our understanding of how certain perplexing entities, particularly contemporary ones, become art. I believe that they are also useful in showing how other quite respectable entities, which we know as artworks, cease being art. I assume here—at least conditional—acceptance of the thesis that entities to which we make ontological commitments as artworks are not the same as entities we experience as objects. Granted this, I can look at some consequences of temporal variations in this relationship. In this regard, I introduce the temporal variables of *begins before, coincides with,* and *endures beyond.* If I take these to be uniformly applicable to "work" and to "object," each relating to the other in one or more of these three ways, I find that there are nine variations on beginnings and ends that mark the possible relationships between the pair.[8] (In note 8 I show how these variations can be schematized.) All these variations, taken together, could provide a novel basis for a categorical scheme of the arts, although it may well be that there are some categories—certain variants in beginnings and ends—for which exemplifying works either do not exist or cannot (yet) be identified.

But my interests here are restricted to the "ends" relationship between works and their objects, and I must forgo the more inclusive consideration of beginnings. Let us assume, for this discussion, an unproblematical construal of beginnings—the one in which beginnings of "works" and of "objects" coincide: $(Wm\text{-}/Om\text{-})$. Given this, my special concern is with the one variation from this group in which *the object endures beyond the work* $(Wm\text{-}/Omz)$. This is the one that presystematically seems most controversial for it brings into question a prized characteristic of artworks, namely, the permanence of their status. I will begin my discussion of this issue in an indirect way by briefly considering the other two variations on endings: where *the ends of the work and the object coincide* (Wmm/Omm), and where *the work endures beyond the object* $(Wmz/Om\text{-})$. Although these may seem somewhat less counterintuitive than the first, they are deceptive in this, and a preliminary look at them may facilitate the approach to my principal subject.

Let us first consider the case where the work endures beyond the object. What, actually, does it mean to say that a work we know of ends? In the *Poetics,* Aristotle refers repeatedly to paintings by artists of his time which are now lost to us and about which, as I gather, we know very little.[9] Yet, in a special way, they could be considered as artworks for we continue to speculate about them, to "reconstruct" them, and to search for their traces in other, extant, works. Of course, such efforts might be dismissed as mere academic gestures or as acts of piety for, as things are, these paintings remain "faceless" and we cannot know, in any satisfactory sense of the term, whether our surmises are true. But this is a matter of evidential adequacy, not ontology, for what we do not know, simply, is enough about what those works "might be (have been) like" to *include* them in our construals of what other works *are* like. However, let us consider another, less remote, example: Suppose—just suppose—that the assault, some years ago, on the Michelangelo *Pietà* had gone much further and the sculpture had been irreparably smashed.[10] A good deal more than piety would encourage continuing to affirm it as a work. In actuality, our acquaintance with visual works is largely indirect for we depend on slides, reproductions, and our memories of infrequently seen originals. Many, if not most, great works of art have never been seen by the people who admire them. Yet such works are "appreciated" and also participate in the appreciation of other works; the *Pietà* influences and enlarges our understanding of, say, Donatello's *Lamentation* or the *Versperbild* in the Ursuline cloister at Erfurt. *This* would not end with the work's physical demise. Before we are tempted to forsake our carefully tended ontologies, however, some qualifications should be added here: One peculiarity of visual works that "survive" their objects is that they are not identical with those earlier works that were "embodied" in these objects. Although "originals" figure less in our conceptions of artworks than we might like, such originals do stand as "correctives" to their facsimiles and to our memories. In principle and in fact we can return to them to refresh ourselves and our theories. Works that are rid of their objects, however, enter into a certain complicity with us: Having lost their role as correctives to our uses of them, they permit us, sometimes too freely, to use them as we wish.

What kind of work would it be, then, that *does* end together with its physical demise? I suppose only one that does not matter to us, that we neither appreciate nor relate to other works. Such unfortunate works are not rare, as can be attested to by the trash bins of studios, galleries, and art schools, and they perhaps can be seen as exemplars of that peculiar theoretical entity: something that is an artwork but has no aesthetic value. The demise of such an entity produces an epistemic nicety—for it is of the kind where we would not know or, presumably, care that the work has ended. The variation being discussed here—where work and object end together—is therefore limitedly instantiated, for it pertains only to the scraps and leavings of art-making, to those things that achieve and lose their status in the half-life between attention and disregard.

III

I return to the issue temporarily laid aside above: the variant of the ends relation between work and object in which *the object endures beyond the work*. The claim that this can occur at all may strike us as somewhat preposterous, for it suggests a state of affairs where some concrete thing that we know to be an artwork somehow relinquishes or loses that status, and this notwithstanding that it remains an object before us. We can imagine standing in the Borghese Palace and looking at, say, Titian's *Sacred and Profane Love*. We might well wonder by what possible alchemy this painting could cease being art short of a sudden and universal affliction of amnesia about the very concept of art. But the improbability felt here, nevertheless, might lead us to wonder about the strength of our feelings and about whether they would be as strong, or as appropriate, in all other situations where artworks are appreciated.

This variation is prima facie neutral about whether the potential for loss of art status is uniformly or selectively predictable of all present works. However, it seems reasonable to assume that, if it applies at all, it applies selectively, if only because our antagonism toward its application increases the more we care about a work. In light of this we would expect that certain artworks—those of great value—are relatively, although perhaps not categorically, exempt from the threat of disenfranchisement. Such valued works can be described as central referents of the overall concept of art and thus as sharing the permanence of the system of beliefs and theories that comprises that concept. In effect, "art" would not be understood as it is—or at all— were these things not known to be artworks. There are many other works, however, that we are less sure about. Such works might be described as relatively peripheral to the system and, correspondingly, as more vulnerable. Such vulnerability, of course, could be taken to correspond only to evaluative judgments—to the "better" and "worse" of artworks—and we may hold that such judgments have no ontological impact at all.[11] Against this, I could argue—as I do above—that to regard a work as having little value is to render it more vulnerable in its status as art, but I admit that I need something stronger than "poor regard" to *guarantee* a work's demise. I need something like the "conflict between accounts" I discuss in the preceding chapter, that is, a withdrawal of attention from the *consideration* of value— for reasons that may themselves be nonaesthetic. I suggest that there are factors other than value—aesthetic or ethical—which are operative in the matter of status and that these factors correspond to certain *nonnormative* interests we have in artworks. I state above that some works are ontically protected by virtue of their "centrality" in our systematic concept of art. These nonnormative factors, then, must be operative together with value, in determinations of centrality. What might some of them be?

One evident protective factor is that the work in question unequivocally exemplifies the formal characteristics that are typically attributed to works of art and especially to visual works. There would be no good reason, therefore, to doubt that this entity, insofar as its symbolic conformation is concerned, both *is* and is *that* artwork. Doubts on this score that would undermine the stability of status usually arise within a context of "antagonism" between art and its social milieu. I describe some such contexts in the preceding chapters, but I suggest there that it is not enough (for loss of status) that something not look (sound, etc.) like art; nor is it enough that something look like a thing that is not art. For something to cease being art it must *be*—as well as look like—something we *do not want* to be art.

Thus, it would seem that works central to the concept of art enjoy an extended social approval, not only through presently held opinion but through layered historical record. Certainly, part of this approval is the measure of a work's aesthetic value; but, importantly, also included is the affirmation of the work's compatibility with nonaesthetic systems of belief, for example, ethical, religious, or political. Thus, the work is not, and has not been, the subject of determinations which, in the larger social context, could override the aesthetic and redefine the work in such a way as to end its status as art.

But there is a factor quite apart from these considerations that, I believe, can create a situation where an object "endures beyond" its work, and this factor is to be found in the relationship between the work and its artist. Let us return, for a moment, to our example of *Sacred and Profane Love*. One thing that protects this painting is our knowledge that the artist—Titian—is no longer alive. Accordingly, if there are any special *rights*[12] that Titian enjoyed as creator of *Sacred and Profane Love*, these rights *no longer* apply. If we argue that only the artist who creates a work has the (aesthetic) right to constitutively change this work, then it would follow that *Sacred and Profane Love* is now aesthetically autonomous relative to any modification that would destroy it either as an artwork or as that specific work. Thus, it seems that there is a privileged relationship between an artist and his work and that it is founded upon a right the artist uniquely enjoys vis-à-vis that work. This brings us directly to the question of status loss. My claim here is that artistic status is contingent upon an artist's construal of a piece as finished. Further, I claim that a positive judgment of "finished" can be *rescinded* in the circumstance that something, properly accepted as an artwork, is recalled by its artist and is revised. When that occurs, the work in question ceases to be the work it formerly was and thereby loses its status as art. It may, however, by *again* being finished, become another work.

A number of immediate problems arise: To call an artwork unfinished seems a contradiction in terms. Whatever it is, in this context, that is unfinished might be identified in the vernacular as a work-in-progress, a rough, an underpainting, and so on, but not as a work as such. Evidently, then, this condition applies only to things that *are* artworks but not to things that "are not yet" or that only "might become" artworks. On the other hand, if—as seems sensible—"being finished" is taken as a necessary condition for "being an artwork," then the conclusion follows that "unfinished" cannot be predicated of artworks.

What is it, however, for an artwork to be finished, and what constitutes knowing whether one is? This is really the same question as asking how an artwork achieves its status and, if one follows the general lines of the "attributing agent" thesis and takes "artist" as a paradigm case of such an agent, the answer would be: "When the artist says it is finished and/or art." The direct evidence of achieved status provided by such statements, on this account, seems to be the strongest criterion of ontic completeness that we have.

IV

This thesis is by no means self-evident, however, and before going further with it I must consider some possible counterarguments. One might insist, for example, that we accept many things as artworks that were not, or were considered not to be, finished by their creators. Examples of such works are Schubert's Eighth Symphony, Kafka's *Castle*, and the many abstract-expressionist paintings whose artists claimed could not—in principle—be finished. We the audience, however, have little difficulty in appreciating these as works notwithstanding the artist's own attitude or premature demise. But appreciation has a broader reach than art status and often embraces all sorts of things that would be excluded by a more strict accounting. Some of these things are quasi works that are "attributed to" an artist and (performances of) works that are "incorrect." Other such things are copies, reproduction, fakes, forgeries, restorations, and defaced works. I submit that unfinished works are part of this fringe and, like the others, often attract our attention and merit our appreciation. Surely, if Brown the bassoonist plays a wrong note in the third movement of the *Eroica*, this alone does not give us reason to say it was a terrible performance, and few of us would insist that the work is, in fact, Brown's first symphony. Like Goodman's criteria for semantic compliance,[13] my distinction here of "finished-unfinished" is *regulatory*, not prescriptive. What we do, or should do, in particular cases is a different matter from that of the ontological determination of a work.

One could further claim, however, that the term "finished" should be used to refer primarily to the characteristics of the works themselves and only secondarily, less consequentially, to their histories of production. On this account a work is finished when it is "enough like" some set of paradigmatic works that gives us the rule for the type. Being "enough like" is here an interpreted resemblance relationship between perceptual characteristics of the work in question and the paradigm works. Because we know, through art-historical evidence, how different sortal-types of artworks look, we can tell whether the work in question belongs to a given type and whether it is an adequate exemplar of that type. This argument seems particularly convincing in the context of ancient art, in cases of obscure or rediscovered works where little is known about their history of production and the only plausible criteria derive from comparisons of perceptual similarities. But the attractions of this argument also point to a number of weaknesses. Apropos works that are historically obscure: An interpretative reliance on perceptual similarities does not work well in *negative* instances. In a situation where the "enough like" relationship between the subject and available models is weak, no adequate distinction can be made between unfinished works and *deviant*, although complete, works.

This difficulty is exacerbated in the context of contemporary art where one could say that deviance from standard forms of art-making has itself become the standard. Here, the criterion of perceptual similarity does not effectively distinguish between finished and unfinished works or, indeed, between works and nonworks. An uncritical reliance on this criterion quickly reduces appreciation to a trivial exercise in taste, an exercise that often obscures the important distinction between aesthetically pleasing objects and artworks. In contrast, I take the claim that a work "looks finished" merely to be confirmatory of independent knowledge that it is finished, that is, merely an indication of one's having learned what some finished works typically look like. Lacking such independent knowledge, however, "looks finished" is a flawed claim, for it confuses a particular work with a type. The work in question, if a work at all, might not be of the type it "looks like" but, rather, might be an unfinished stage of a different type. Basing the ontic status of a work on purely perceptual evidence, then, identifies neither work nor type but only a stereotype.

V

I offer the thesis about works by artists who are still alive, that their status as works remains insecure during the life span of the artist. The reason for this, as I indicate above, is that an artist can change his mind and decide that a work of his is in fact unfinished, and this notwithstanding that he had previously affirmed its completeness by exhibiting it, selling it, and so forth. The question immediately arises: Why should we not take such a decision in all cases simply to be the righting of a previous error? Sometimes, of course, it is, but I submit that there are other cases where we cannot take it as an error, cases where a bona fide status loss occurs.

This premise is based on two considerations: The first concerns the privileged relations that artists have with their own works; the second has to do with the ontological fortunes of works when they are "independent of" the artist. To show this I offer a scenario comparing an artist's actions vis-à-vis his own works with possible actions of others. For example: Being an artist, I make a work—a painting—and when I am satisfied with it I project it publicly by sending it off to an exhibition. After it is returned to my studio, I look at it again, see things I want to change, and proceed to paint on it further. That I have a perfect right to do so seems evident, but the relative status of the two entities—the "earlier" and "later" painting—is not as evident. Let me compare this with a different example: The painting I put on exhibition was sold but, alas, to someone who subsequently decided he did not like it and proceeded to repaint it. Although the original painting is legally his property, his aesthetic right to alter it, unlike mine, is not without question. I can retaliate by exercising the right I have that corresponds to the one of status-conferring. I can withdraw such status. I can proclaim to all who will listen that my erstwhile work is now aesthetically valueless, not a work at all but merely colored grease, wood, and canvas. If my antagonist is himself not an artist, my retaliation here is most effective, for his act of painting on my work is then only an act of desecration. But what if he were another artist? Then I could say of the changed work only that it is not my work but not that it is not a work at all, for it may be that, like Rauschenberg's erased de Kooning, it has become another (his) work.

Now, except for possible differences in public reaction, might we not say that this last situation is essentially the same as the one in which I repaint my own painting? In both cases we seem to have a work that ceases to be by virtue of an artist's action that transforms it into another work. But there must remain some difference between the provenance that an artist has over his own work and the provenance that someone else, even another artist, has over that work. Of course, in actual cases, aesthetic rights are inevitably tempered by aesthetic values. In the "two artists–two works" situation it would matter a great deal if I were Balthus and the "repainter" a disgruntled, although wealthy, expressionist; and conversely—at least these days—if I were Fabritius and he Rembrandt. But an artist's provenance over his own work has a singular cast to it. If Picasso in his last years bought back, say, the

Portrait of Kahnweiler and repainted it, there might indeed be protest over the loss of a masterpiece—whatever else was produced. But only Picasso could give as a reason for doing so that he considered the work unfinished. Of course, once having made such a decision he need not then have physically altered the painting to confirm its loss of status. "Finishing" the painting is only *one* possible consequence of the determination that it is unfinished; after so deciding, the artist could just as well have left the painting alone.

Someone can make a finished work of mine into another work, in which case we have two works—his and mine—although mine may be "under" the one that is his. Someone can find something I have not completed and assert that it is a finished work; but then, even if he attributes it to me, there is only one work: his. However, only I can say of a finished work of mine that it is unfinished. In this case, however, do we have one work or none?

This question really concerns the relationship between the two determinations, the earlier and the later. Does not the second one of "incompleteness" contravene the first one of "completeness"? I assume here, without arguing, that the function of "completing" is cumulative and temporally unidirectional and that its reversal is not "incompleting" but, rather, "dismantling" or "destroying." In what sense, then, could I assert that something I earlier completed is now incomplete, without implying that earlier I was mistaken? As an answer, I suggest that there can be another relationship between these two determinations besides the one of contravention. The second determination need not show the first to have been in error but, instead, can terminate the applicability of the first, at the time of the second, to the perceptual object in question. Thus, we do have one work rather than no works, although that work is now a *nonconcrete theoretic entity*[14]—for the status of artwork was withdrawn from the concrete object at the time it was determined to be incomplete.

This raises a troubling question about the grounds for the second determination. Are they the same as those for the first? If we hold that the first was not mistaken and also that, so long as the criteria remain the same, "incompleteness" cannot properly be posited of a thing previously judged to be complete, then we must conclude that the criteria have changed between the two determinations. This conclusion could jeopardize the entire argument being made here, for it seems to invalidate any other claims—for example, of status loss—that require consistent criteria for their determinations. But I suggest that the problem here is not with inconsistencies between instances of determination but with our concept of "sameness" between works.

VI

Apropos this distinction between "concrete" and "theoretic" works, I refer again to Margolis's concept of "embodiment"[15] and to one of the stipulated conditions, namely, that a work has certain properties that its embodying object does not have. My thesis here, like that of Margolis, requires a distinction between "work" and "object," but I interpret the nature of this distinction in another way. Although Margolis identifies "work" and "object" as separate conceptual entities, he does not construe them as separate existents. He nowhere speaks, for example, of "dis-embodied" works although, of course, he admits to objects that are "non-embodiers."

The shortcomings of Margolis's thesis, for me, lie precisely where he seems to find its greatest strength, that is, in his contention that the embodiment relationship is one of neither identity nor duality—that works and their objects are identical in extension although distinct in other (intensional) properties. Of course, entities may be characterized any number of ways without requiring that each characterization be a separate "embodiment" within that entity. One can construe something as a painting, a possession, a tax shelter, or colored grease on canvas, and take all these merely to be different descriptions of one self-identical object, and while some such descriptions may be preferred at different times, none is inapplicable at any given time. Margolis, as we know, wants more. He holds that because artworks are conventional entities, they are ontologically underspecified by their physical descriptions. Thus, as embodied works have properties that their objects do not—indeed, "cannot"—have, Margolis takes the considerable risk of placing embodiment on the precarious perch between identity and duality. On the whole, I am sympathetic with Margolis's efforts, for I believe that distinctions of the kind he makes are crucial in safeguarding the concept of art from the barbarities of reductionism. I also believe, however, that his conceptual "balancing act" in this regard is unnecessary. The threat of dualism can be avoided by taking the position, as I do, that the differential provided by the embodiment thesis does not require the coextensiveness of work and object. I argue here that the beginnings and ends of works and their objects need do no more than overlap, that either may end before or endure beyond the other. The risk in my own thesis is thus with a further proliferation of entities, for in order to account for "disembodied works" and "disenfranchised objects," I divide the concept of artwork into "concrete" and "theoretic" aspects.

One problem with my proposal is the claim that a nonconcrete entity occurs in a sense that implies its existence. This, admittedly, points to a weaker sense of "occur" than an empirical theory would ordinarily want for an existence claim. I am not sure, at this point, as to the precise construal of "occur" that my argument requires. It seems to me, however, that between the sense of "exist" that is strong enough for concrete entities and one that is too weak for cultural or theoretic entities, there is a gray area in which I may be able to find the version that I need. Certainly, a theoretic work does not exist like Dr. Johnson's "chair," but to say that it exists as does George Washington "in the hearts of his countrymen" seems too weak. Margolis models his work-object relationship on the one that holds between "persons" and "physical bodies."[16] There are some differences between these pairs that should be considered, however. A photographic reproduction is more like the painting that it images than is an image of a person like that person; we do not, for example, call a person's picture a "reproduction." Also, a "quote" of another artist's painting that I include in my painting is more like the painting quoted than is a grandson's incarnation of his grandfather like that grandfather. Yet, the works that are "in" the reproduction and the quote need not be concrete. Another consideration: A work's identity as art seems more dependent upon a specification of antecedent works to which it is constitutively similar than is one's identity as a person dependent upon causal inference to particular parents. Also, unlike persons, an artwork's identity additionally seems to depend upon positing works in the future that will be constitutively similar to it. Seen these ways, works exist in their antecedents and descendants in a stronger sense than persons can be said to exist in their forebears and offspring. I suggest that such "enabling" relations between artworks are not limited to "embodied" or concrete works but also extend to include theoretic, "disembodied" works as well. How cogently any such works can be said to "exist" by virtue of these relationships depends upon how we generally construe existence claims for cultural or conventional entities; *that* depends, in turn, upon how best we can account for them and what we want of them.

VII

My proposal, then, is for a more radical relativization of the concept of artwork than is given by Margolis. I distinguish two existentially separable aspects: a *concrete* one and a *theoretic* one. A work may originate—and terminate—in its concrete aspect, but it may endure solely in its theoretic one. Termination of status in the concrete aspect need not negate the accrued theoretic status. A work that is concrete is the work embodied in an object; it is an entity that can be accounted for in physical, perceptual, and cultural (contextual) terms. The theoretic work, on the other hand, is a work "rid of" its object; it is an entity that continues to have a history and, therefore, a contextual description, but, as it is not concrete, it has no physical description. Perceptually, a theoretic work can be said to have "referred" characteristics, for it exists as traces of its concrete aspect in the perceptual characteristics of other concrete works and in its own reproductions or copies.

In chapter 6 I present a detailed description of the process through which things become known as artworks, and I develop my description into an ontological theory.[17] As this theory has bearing on my present discussion, I outline it briefly here: I hold that the status of a work is located in the works it is seen to resemble and that resemble it; in works that it influences and is influenced by; in actual works that it takes to be its "antecedents" and in hypothetical works that it anticipates will be its "consequents." In the discussion of this interpretative nexus or "tradition class" to which artworks belong, I use the metaphorical device of personification and thereby describe the conditions of class formation and membership as being dependent on volitions of the works themselves. In this account, candidate objects "designate" those antecedent works that "confirm" that they are consequentially alike. Such confirmation is based upon the hypothesis that future works of merit also will have these consequential characteristics and thus justify the formation of this, rather than another, tradition class. Thus, the category "theoretic work" further divides, for it now contains all those antecedent (historical) works we know whose physical aspects have been lost or destroyed. Also to be counted as theoretic are those I call "future works," which, as they are only projections of what later (concrete) works might be like, do not, as yet, have physical aspects. One consequence of this theory is that destroyed concrete works, though no longer the objects they once were, may endure—as theoretic works—by virtue of their inclusion in the interpretation of other works. Another consequence of particular import for the present chapter is that works that are determined by their artists to be incomplete cease being works in their concrete aspect and therefore may justly be reworked, but they endure as works in their theoretic aspect—in this case also through their inclusion in interpretations of other works. The determination of incompleteness has ontological sway *only* over the concrete work in that the artist's rights are limited to this aspect. An artist cannot, for example, "expunge" consideration of his work from the interpretations of other works, although his conviction that this (concrete) work is now incomplete will undoubtedly modify its (theoretic) role in those interpretations.

If this argument is sound, I can hold, without inconsistency, that the criteria for the determination of a work's completeness remain constant between times, that (*a*) the same *form* of determination is applied to a work in the earlier and later instance, and (*b*) neither *instance* of determination need be a mistake. In the context of this discussion, the work that is first "complete" and later "incomplete" is the same concrete object; but it is *not* the same theoretic entity for, between the two instances, it has come to be included in, and perhaps *rejected from*, the interpretations of other works, that is, the formation of other tradition classes. Although the determination of incompleteness applies to the concrete aspect, it is consequent upon the theoretic aspect, for this aspect, unlike the concrete one, *does* change between times. It is to *this* aspect that the artist refers, for it provides the *reasons* for judging the concrete work to be incomplete.

The objection might be raised here that this emphasis on the artist's provenance over his work permits mockery or absurdity, for what would safeguard a work (or us) from a spate of consecutive and ongoing affirmations and denials? But we must remember that the status in question is a conventional one, and evidence for its proper application is found through a comparison with other attributive acts. Some of this evidence is surely intentional, for we want to know if the artist is "sincere," if he is indeed in that febrile state where three-second intervals are time enough for mind-changing, or if he is a fraud and is merely deceiving us. This matter actually need not concern us, for the artist and his anxious work are a sufficient pair for the formal determination of status. But if the matter is public, then the onus falls on the artist—or a surrogate critic—to present evidence strong enough to override the seeming unreasonableness of the situation. The testing of "intentions" through ancillary evidence is common to all our social and legal interchanges, and the interpretation of artworks should provide no exception. Public acquiescence in a claim of art status contributes to establishing a work's theoretic aspect; it acknowledges the work's participation in a tradition class. Sometimes we come to doubt the legitimacy of such a claim because the conditions under which it was made do not support it. Sometimes, like some artists, we change our minds.

Whether or not we accept a particular attributive act as genuine, however, it seems clear that, taken in their concrete aspect, artworks maintain their status only precariously in the lifetime of the artist; in principle, they are all subject to its withdrawal by virtue of being considered incomplete. Whether, in practice, this results in a revising, or a discarding, or is only an exercise in imagination depends on other, often nonaesthetic, factors. But the verdict of incompleteness, as I describe it here, presents us with a bona fide case where the object endures beyond the work.

SIX

A Basis for Attributions of "Art"

In the preceding chapters, my discussions, however varied, present a common theme: that matters of "art" are to be understood as a context of interactions between physical and conceptual entities, and that all particular judgments—ontological, historical, normative—derive from and are each partial determinants of this context. In this chapter, I attempt to make this theme explicit by describing how this "context of interactions" actually works. In doing this, I measure my thesis against some others along a spectrum of agreements and disagreements. A number of theorists have influenced my thinking in this area; I have remarked on some of Joseph Margolis's ideas in chapter 5, and here I discuss some theories of George Dickie and Arthur Danto.

For purposes of orientation, I need a label, an umbrella term, that distinguishes a direction of theory I am sympathetic to and that permits me to make broad distinctions between this and other theories before I proceed to the specific distinctions that identify my own thinking. I offer the term "contextual theory" for this purpose. As this is a term of convenience, I do not propose that it designate a category "in re," nor do I insist on its appropriateness for those theories of others with which I essentially agree.

One of the virtues of a contextualist approach to art lies in the thesis that the status "art" and attributions of that status are independent of any particular aggregate of perceived qualities or conceived properties. Whether we take the attributive act to occur within the general context of a "theory" of art, as Arthur Danto holds,[1] or through the individual gesture of a "representative" of the artworld, as George Dickie has it,[2] in neither case do we require the "candidate" for art status to conform with any antecedent categorical set of attributes—whether of beauty, significance, expressiveness, or any other—upon which the determination is to be based. In this sense, contextual theory seems to be most deeply linked with modernism and, in particular, with art of the avant-garde, for it effectively accounts for the many new and radical works which, in retrospect, indubitably are art but which did not offer, in their respective candidacies, such distinguishing earmarks as were then known to be possessed by all and only artworks. Yet, a contextualist approach also presents some difficulties which, in this chapter, I propose to analyze and to which I offer some correctives of my own.

Before I continue with the discussion of these difficulties, however, it might be useful to look at an aesthetic viewpoint that contextual theory, whatever its internal variations, is opposed to. In this way, the significance of these difficulties for the later discussions may become clearer. The viewpoint to which I refer contains the familiar thesis that entities are known to be art by virtue of the *exhibited qualities* they possess.

My concern here is not to study or compare particular theories that contain this thesis. Rather, I focus on certain salient features that, historically and ideologically, compose an opposing view to contextualism. Accordingly, I introduce another umbrella term, "exhibited qualities theory," and I use it as a label for those theories that hold that all and only artworks possess and exhibit certain special qualities, the recognition of which is an essential component in their achievement of status, that is, in determinations that they are art.[3] Here, I call these qualities "artistic" qualities to distinguish between them and the "aesthetic" qualities which other things that are not art may possess, and to underline the contention that things are art by virtue of having—because they have—such qualities. A major criterion for this theory is that the qualities adduced function as determinations of artworks and not merely as their post-factum descriptions.

In one sense, this exhibited qualities thesis is but the converse of the contextualist one in which the determination—that something is art—provides the basis for deciding which characteristics are artistically relevant. The tension between these two theses can be indicated by the following question: Is it the epistemic function of a set of qualities to *determine*, through some process of "matching," which candidate objects are indeed artworks, or does such a set arise as a *consequence* of determinations otherwise made whereby it serves only as a partial *description* of what is already held to be art? In the former case, the possession of certain qualities is taken as a prerequisite for the status of artwork rather than merely as a basis for adjudicating between things that already are art. Such possession takes on predictive force: As the relevant qualities configurate into arrays, they become compliants of such standard generic terms as "beauty," "significant form," and so on. These generics, in turn, are accepted as the sufficient conditions for art.

One of the major problems for the qualities thesis is caused by the purported artwork that possesses none, or not enough, of the requisite qualities. One response to this problem would be the philosophically risky one of modifying the qualities array so as to include those of the new piece. But such a move, as it is essentially reactive, compromises the predictive force the theory claims for itself. Of course, there is always another alternative: The drawbridge may be raised, and the offending piece deemed mere trivia, an unfortunate example of contextualist "permissiveness"—not really art at all. This second move is also risky, especially within an avant-garde context. Adherence to a thesis of eternal artistic qualities—even generalized, as Monroe Beardsley does with his "regional qualities"—goes against the sense of discontinuity and disaffection that characterizes much new art.

In their writings, both Danto and Dickie discuss a variety of new and "radical" works in ways that exacerbate the difficulties of the qualities thesis. These discussions chronicle the ongoing assaults on standard aesthetic categories that typify the art in question. Danto introduces quiddities and oddities of artworks, real and imagined, that confound the boundaries between art and nonart. He justifies his preferences by indicating that it is these and not other, "safer" works that are consequential (in a somewhat Hegelian sense) for present aesthetic theory.[4] Dickie's examples (e.g., Duchamp's "urinal") have been singled out for the criticism that such works are marginal and eccentric and are therefore to be discounted as defeating conditions for antecedent formulations of artistic qualities.[5] In response to this, Dickie argues effectively that, within the ontology of artifacts, no natural subdivision can be found that sorts out artworks and that, therefore, "anything can become art."[6] Danto's analysis of the attribution of "art" adds strength to this argument. He posits an inevitable new work, not defeatable as art, which will be such that the schema of predicates presently coextensive with "——— is art" cannot be used to affirm it. This work, when actual, functions to add a new predicate to this schema upon which the expanded schema is applicable not only to the new work but, retroactively, to all other (historical) works.

The contrast between contextual and exhibited qualities theories in the matter of determining artworks is, thus, also a contrast in attitudes toward avant-garde art. This contrast does not fall out neatly, of course, for the variations within each approach are considerable. I suggest, however, that a qualities aesthetic would want some minimal correlation between the criteria upon which the appreciations of extant valued works and novel presumptive works are based. This is because these criteria identify the exhibited qualities such appreciation is "of," and discerning them provides the distinction between legitimate and illegitimate candidates. Contextual theory, as I indicate, does not have this correlation. Indeed, a salient feature of this approach is its indifference to specifications of "what art should be like." But there are problems here too, for, if there are no specifications, we might easily conclude that "anything can be art." Yet, we know that not everything is, and evidently most things will not be. There is a need, then, for contextual theorists to give an alternative account of how things come to be art, one that is not based upon "recognition of qualities" but that is able to provide the wanted discriminations. In section II, I discuss the account given by George Dickie.

II

As I understand it, Dickie's account of the attributive process rests upon three main points. (1) *Artifactuality*: One requirement for the status of artwork is that something be an artifact. (2) *Two "senses" of art*: A thing may be considered an artwork in the classificatory sense, which merely identifies a subcategory of artifacts; a thing may also be considered an artwork in the evaluative sense, which ranks the entities in that subcategory according to criteria of artistic value. (3) *Candidate-agent*: The status of art is conferred on a candidate artifact by an agent acting on behalf of an institution known as the artworld.[7]

Each of these criteria provides some measure of difficulty for Dickie's thesis. The least of these, which I shall discuss only in passing, is the criterion of artifactuality (1). Holding to this criterion excludes much work that derives from historical avant-garde intersections between "objects" and "actions"—for example, performance art, happenings, conceptual art. Expanding the criterion of artifactuality to include human actions, however, only makes it so broad as to be superfluous. Looking more closely, we may also wonder what precisely distinguishes an artifact from a "natural" object. Is it enough for "artifacture," for example, that I "notice" a sea stone in a certain way? Or must I remove it from the shore and isolate it, say, on a pedestal? Need I also polish it? But what if I exhibit it as it lies, among its companions, and invite my friends to the opening? This criterion, unfortunately, serves mainly as a target for irreverence.

Dickie's second criterion, the one that separates classification and value into independent functions, gives me the most difficulty. I believe it to be an untenable thesis which, perhaps, is prompted by the hope that value determinations, separately, will provide the exclusiveness that classifying does not and will thereby save the status of art in this theory from triviality. But the theory cannot do this through the assigned separateness. In fact, this thesis undermines the third of Dickie's criteria, that of candidate-agent. I begin my analysis with this third criterion and develop my objections to the classification/value distinction as I proceed.

In looking at Dickie's scenario of an "agent of the artworld" conferring status on a "candidate object," certain questions arise: What grounds do we have for distinguishing between candidates and noncandidates? Are there, for example, "artable" things that, nevertheless, are not eligible for that status? Are all candidates successful? Is to be a candidate also to be an artwork, or are there some candidates that fail and remain artifacts? One notices that the tense these questions are couched in—the "eternal present"—trivializes the issue. We know, both at any given moment and viewed timelessly, the world is such that some eligible things are not candidates and some candidates are not artworks. Perhaps the tense needs changing, for I submit that it is the process—the "rites of passage" between identities—that matters here. So I rephrase these questions: We want to know why all eligible things do not become candidates and whether all candidates become artworks. We want to know what *values* underly the decisions being made. In order to clarify some of the main points of controversy, I now look more closely at the positions I have outlined thus far. What follows is a somewhat technical discussion which, if bypassed, can be retrieved from later sections.

I use the following notations as aids in identifying the main threads of the argument:

W = df. "———— is art" ("is an artwork").
A = df. "———— is eligible for the status of artwork."
C = df. "———— is a candidate for the status of artwork."
Q = df. "———— has those properties that are interpreted as artistic qualities."
$t, t + 1, t + 2$: Individual variables ranging over times; e.g., t refers to a nonfixed present, $t + 1$ to a time later than t, $t + 2$ to a time later than $t + 1$.

It seems to me that in attempting to ascertain the conditions under which the term "art" is attributed to things, we need to identify the sequence of events that comprise such attributions. This would involve a temporal ordering of the predications that make up—that are considered consequential in—attributive acts. Above, I outline one such set of predicates: W, A, C, Q. In the discussion that follows, those predications which are mutually implicative, that is, whose relationship is expressed by the biconditional, I interpret as describing states of affairs that occur at the same time, t. When the implication is unidirectional, that is, is expressed as a simple conditional, the predicates thus related are interpreted as applying at different times: t, $t + 1$. Accordingly, when we consider an attributive theory such as presented earlier—that things are art by virtue of possessing certain determinate artistic qualities—the following possibilities obtain: If we specify that all and only such things as possess these qualities can be art, we are saying that "having qualities," Q, and "being eligible," A, are both applicable to things at the same time, t. We are also saying that there is nothing to which Q applies to which A does not also apply. Thus Q and A, reciprocally, are here interpreted as sufficient conditions for each other's applicability. However, if our theory further specifies that not everything that is eligible becomes an artwork, then we are saying that A is implied by but does not imply W. Accordingly, if W applies to something at $t + 1$, then A applies to that thing at t; but there may be something A at t that is not W at $t + 1$. The theory thus presented fails to specify fully the conditions under which things that can be, become art, for it does not give the sufficient conditions for the application of W.

Of course, we could take the more extreme view that Q, A, and W are *all* mutually implicative and thus are all applicable at t. In this case we would be saying that all those things that possess the specified qualities *are* artworks, and thereby we effectively eliminate the need for the intermediary predication of A. But this view does not give us much of an attributive theory, only a—probably circular—definition of art. But such a definition, circular or not, does not provide us with what I believe counts for a coherent attributive theory: a delineation of the *sequence of events* within which we differentiate things that are and are not art. This sequence should include the successive intermediaries of (*a*) things that can be but will not be art, and (*b*) things that both can be and become art.

In the thesis that affirms the temporal difference in the applicability of A and W, we find that A is not superfluous if it functions to distinguish between things that are eligible for the status of art and things that are not. When it does so, we see that the concept of "work" is not parasitic on the concept of "candidacy"; that is, nothing is both A and W at t, and not everything that is A at t is W at $t + 1$. But there is a further problem: We have seen this theory also to state that things are A by virtue of being Q. Of course, we can assume here that anything which is an artwork has artistic qualities, but we also know that, for contextual theory, such qualities are determinable only at the time when W applies: at $t + 1$. The reason is that from the vantage point of A (at t), we do not know what qualities count for W (at $t + 1$) because we cannot then know which of the things that are eligible will become works. On the other hand, from the vantage point of W (at $t + 1$), we can say only that the qualities of a work may include, but need not be limited to, the qualities ascribed to it before it was a work (at t). Here the reason is that inasmuch as works presumably are distinguishable from things that are not (yet) works, the qualities that describe works compose either an alternative set to or a more comprehensive set than the qualities set that accounts for potential works. I argue that to move from the instance at which A is predicable to that at which W is predicable requires of our theory something other than the application of a coextensive Q at both t and $t + 1$.

One interpretation of the process of attribution that provides this "something other" is found in Dickie's writings on this issue. Dickie limits his assertion, "anything can be art," to the realm of artifacts, but he takes the range of A, within that realm, to be universal. Dickie's differential between A and W—between the inclusive set of artifacts and the exclusive set of artworks—is provided by the predicate C, "——— is a candidate for art status." With the introduction of C, the importance of Q for A is weakened, for now nothing is required of a thing that is A other than it be an artifact. "Artifactuality," however, does not function here as a quality; rather, it serves only to identify the "universe of discourse" for the theory. The question as to what qualities might be shared by all and only artifacts becomes irrelevant; and specifications of qualities that artworks possess are taken only as the ex post facto *consequences* of their achievement of artistic status. Therefore, Q, in this new context, is merely descriptive and not determinative. This is the essential distinction I draw between a qualities and a contextualist position.

Although, in Dickie's theory, the predicate C replaces Q as the mediator between A and W, there are problems that arise here as well. It is evident that not all artifacts become "candidates for appreciation" and, therefore, we can say that though C implies A, A does not imply C. A differential is still needed between those artifacts that do and those that do not become candidates. A further question concerns the relationship here between C and W. It is not clear to me, in Dickie's formulation of "candidacy," whether or not C and W are mutually implicative—whether to be a candidate is *already* to be an artwork—or whether there are candidates that *fail* to become artworks. In the first interpretation, the status of artwork does not seem fairly won, for inasmuch as success is assured the concept of artwork is here parasitic on that of candidate. In the second interpretation, where this is not the case, a differential is still needed between those candidates that do and those that do not succeed in becoming artworks—in my terminology, between C and W.

We can take Dickie's thesis of "agent of the artworld" as providing the earlier differential between A and C, for it is certainly by virtue of an agent's designating act that certain artifacts and not others become candidates for appreciation. But if we use an agent's act to mediate between A and C, can we also use it to mediate between C and W—in the interpretation where their relationship is nonparasitic? Dickie nowhere suggests that two separate acts might occur in this phase of an attribution or even that the single act might be an extended, composite one. But, then, it would seem that either the concept of candidacy is redundant in his theory or the problem remains of how to distinguish between successful and unsuccessful candidates.

In order to restate this problem in my formal terminology, I say that only those artifacts (things that are A at t) become candidates (C at $t + 1$) that are so designated by an agent of the artworld. When I also hold that C and W are not mutually implicative, that is, that not all candidates become artworks, I further distinguish between C at $t + 1$ and W at $t + 2$. The problem here is to explain the basis upon which this latter distinction is made.

I now return to the issue of Dickie's attributive theory. The vagueness, in this theory, of the concept of candidacy seems to me to be linked with his other thesis—that of the "two senses" of the term "artwork." As I indicate in section II, Dickie holds that this term has two forms of application: the "classificatory" and the "evaluative." The first of these seems to designate something like "artwork as such" and thereby to distinguish only between those things that have such status and those that do not. The second sense presumably operates within the realm identified by the first solely by sorting out artworks on some basis of relative value or merit. Dickie states that the evaluative sense is the one "customarily" employed in practice and that the classificatory "rarely" is. He also states, however, that the classificatory sense is "necessary" as it is a "basic concept that structures and guides our thinking about the aesthetic."[8] It is not clear whether Dickie means his two senses to provide a purely theoretical distinction—a parsing of unified practice into its formal components—or whether he means them to indicate distinctions actually made through practices. Certainly, "customarily" and "rarely" have an empirical ring to them; they sound as if they refer to actual states of affairs, as if there are or could be entities that do not have—or do not show—any artistic value but that, nevertheless, we know to be artworks. One wonders here what such things would be like.

It seems to me that the transition from the status of candidate to that of artwork cannot ultimately be explained on any other basis than that of *assigned* value, and the transition of a thing to the status of candidacy can be explained only on the basis of *assignable* value. On what other basis could an unsuccessful candidate be rejected? And why else would something be accepted for candidacy? This argues against the possibility of a purely classificatory attribution.

But what does my own thesis of a unified status-value determination come to? Why is it that we must assess a thing's value even as we ask whether it is art? I give a detailed answer to these questions in the following section, but I introduce the topic here through a—mostly fictional—example: One day I announce to my class, deeply mired as it is in the ontological bogs, that I have with me an artwork for perusal and discussion. I then point to the brief-case I had just placed on the table. One virtue of a philosophy class is that its students tend to be wise in different ways; the immediate impulse to say "But that's your briefcase" is checked, and they wait to see what I'm up to. Referring to past discussions, I insist that I am a perfectly plausible "agent of the artworld," that my status-conferring act is thereby valid, and, ergo, that my "briefcase-work" is authentically art. Also, to "strengthen" my case, I remark on the qualities to be found in the object's battered surfaces and lumpy shape. Thereupon, one student states that her father has a similar briefcase, that she prefers the smooth plastic and slim lines of the one she owns, and that, anyhow, one can find qualities to appreciate in almost any-thing without confusing the issue with "art." I reply that my evocation of qualities was meant to make acceptance of my claim easier but that, in fact, my status-conferring act is prior to appreciation. Another student then ac-cuses me of a tired "Duchampian" ploy which, in "today's" context, no longer even has conceptual novelty, and the student further asserts that my "candidate piece" is not an artwork at all but a fake. I have nothing I can say to this. A third, more subdued student then asks me whether this briefcase is not the same one I recently exhibited in the "semiannual, local-artists show." Now that I see the cat is out and running, I attempt to set the matter straight. The briefcase is not really an artwork, say I; my claim to the con-trary is merely a pedagogical move—to dramatize the issue of ontological status. As to the exhibition: Being somewhat cynical about such affairs, I merely used it to add complexity to my presentation of this issue. I am then told that a number of young artists were much impressed with my "briefcase-work"—a welcome relief, as they said, from all the still lifes—and that one such artist is embarking on a project of his own, a "narrative as-semblage," incorporating briefcases of many shapes, sizes, and states of repair. Further, this artist acknowledges my piece as a source of inspiration.

It seems that both as artist and as agent I have lost jurisdiction in the mat-ter of status. My piece now exists as art through the strength of its relation-ship with the later, "assemblage" work, whereas, earlier, it failed as art through the weakness of its evocation of Duchamp. My early assertion that the briefcase is art was not enough to secure it that status, and my later denial of this assertion was not enough to rescind that status, once achieved. How do I explain this? Perhaps, to begin with, in the following way: Between its earlier and later presentations, the credibility of my candidate's claim to status had changed. This change recast the relationship between my candidate and the artworld through its affirmation of a mutual dependency between the candidate and a class of artworks. Establishing this dependency provided the *valuational* basis for the candidate's status as art. I can now put this into a more propositional form: I claim that attributing "art" to a candidate entails estimating the *consequentiality* of a class of artworks that includes the candidate relative to a class that excludes it or to a class that includes a different candidate. In section III of this chapter, I offer an analysis of what this "estimate of consequentiality" comes to.

III

To begin the discussion, I offer the thesis that the status of artwork is achieved through a transaction between certain specific entities, all of which stand to gain or lose by the outcome of that transaction. Of course, the real entities that stand so to gain and lose are people; evidently, what artworks are comes to our uses of them. But this approach to the problem spawns both irrelevancies and tedium. Much as we do not know how far the artworld extends, so we do not know who among us is or is not a part of it, and finding out is, at best, a thankless task. Also, were we to know these limits, and to argue from them, we would need to deflect our talk about artworks to talk about actions of human agents. But this mires us in sociology and prevents us from giving a direct account (although metaphorical) of the entities that incontestably belong to the artworld—the works themselves. So, in order to avoid the indirectness of sociological descriptions, I conceive of the transaction noted above as occurring between the works themselves. Within this conception, works are sorted out along a temporal matrix and, correspondingly, the transaction is seen as taking place between entities that *are*, *will be*, and *aspire to be* art. By thus personifying these entities I deal directly with the criteria for their relationship without attempting to locate these criteria within the actual—human—constituency of the artworld. However, through this metaphorical account of artworks anthropomorphically engaging each other—as *predecessors*, *candidates*, and *successors*—I do provide the form that any such engagement must take.

My main thesis, as I state it above, is that functions of status attribution, that is, "——— is an artwork," and functions of value attribution, that is, "——— has (some measure of) artistic value," are not separable in any instance of a candidacy. If, for example, I were to interpret artworks as (timelessly) constituting a "class," I would then hold that the status of a work is defined through its position of consequence, relative to other works, in the complex hierarchy that exemplifies such a class. On the other hand, within a temporal description of an attribution, I hold instead that the status of art-work is achieved through a "claim" made by a candidate object: that it provides a valuable *link* between a group of antecedent works and a projected "future work," and that because of this link its own candidacy should be sup-ported. I argue that neither "artistic status" nor "artistic value" can be held as the sole primitive in an adequate attributive theory. I take the contrary position that descriptive contexts are *completely permeated* by the evalua-tive and that attributing "art" to an object is also a projection of that object's *consequentiality* as measured by the support it "gives to," and "asks of," other works of art. On this account, antecedent works do not escape the consequences of a present attribution, nor are future works independent of it. Putting the matter thus indicates that the import of an attribution of art is relational; it expresses the status of a work in terms of its value for the status of other works. The consequences, for a group of works, of supporting some-thing as art are also incurred by the candidate object, so that as regards all constituents the evaluative function is reciprocal. For something to be a candidate for art status, it must, in some acceptable empirical sense, exist at some time; but the measure of its status as a work of art may change even when, as a concrete object, it *no longer* exists. Additionally, something may alter the status of an actual work through the status it enjoys as a projected work even though, as a concrete object, it *does not (yet)* exist. The valua-tional nature of a present attribution can be seen in the fact that past attribu-tions, themselves "value-laden," are never complete even though the work in question may be destroyed. How consequential one takes past artworks to be depends, generally speaking, upon what kinds of things one chooses as art in the present, and this in turn depends upon what one expects artworks to be like in the future. The interdependency here is fairly complex—certainly in the actual fabric of decision making, but also in the formal nature of such relationships.

The relationship between past, or "antecedent," works and present candi-dates may be described as symmetrical. There is a consideration of a request for support and an anticipation that, if it is given, support of another kind will be reciprocated. The request begins with a declaration that the candidate object and the antecedent works applied to share certain significant charac-teristics; that is, they are similar in some important ways. The granting of the candidate's request—the recognition that it is significantly "like" certain past works—is one received part of the transaction, from the vantage point of the present. What must in turn be tendered by the candidate to the antecedent works is some assurance that their value will, at the least, not decrease and perhaps will increase over what it was prior to their having given that candidate support.

In this description of the conditions of interchange—the giving and receiving that comprise determinations of status—a balance must be achieved between levels of aspiration and levels of support. I strike this balance by looking in the other direction, by expanding the decision context to include the future. I hypothesize that, within the class of all artworks, there is some work, *not yet made*, that stands in a special relationship to the others involved in a candidacy. This work, taken timelessly, "has" certain characteristics and a determinate value; and it functions to make credible the promise by the present candidate to an antecedent group of works: that they will benefit by lending the candidate their support. Such credibility is extractable from the thesis that, inasmuch as the future work *is* valuable, a linkage effected between it and those past works will work to their advantage; that is, it will enhance their value. The role of the present candidate in this matching is to be seen in its offer of aid. The proposal it makes to the antecedent works whose support it enlists is that, by their accepting *it* into a *successor* relationship with them, their chances of entering into a *predecessor* relationship with the future (valuable) work will be *improved*.

The candidate, in asking for support, identifies itself through a set of characteristics which, it asserts, are similar to some characteristic set of the antecedent works. If those works *accept* this claim of similarity, they will be provided, so the proposal goes, with a link to the future work. The set of characteristics for which the candidate asks support is one which it *also* claims to be in a similarity relationship with the set of characteristics upon which the value of the future work is based. The candidate work, in this way, offers itself as *evidence* for accepting a particular construal of artistic value. It predicts, in effect, that the characteristics upon which its own candidacy is based will come to be recognized as artistically valuable because some valuable future work will possess similar characteristics. The antecedent works, by accepting these characteristics into their own description (and thereby lending support to the candidate), will be rewarded by a future corroboration that these are, indeed, the consequential characteristics in a temporally extended—historical—scheme of artistic value.

I use the term "tradition class" to stand for a temporal class of designated works whose members assume the status, vis-à-vis each other, of antecedent, candidate, and future work. This designation, as I indicate above, is the candidate's self-presentation to those antecedent works through the thesis exemplified by the future work: that together they constitute a cogent and valuable reification of art-historical process. The acceptance of this thesis by the designated antecedent works affirms the class to be so constituted.

There is no guarantee, of course, that anything of the kind described in this thesis will actually be the case, that there actually is such a tradition class, inasmuch as there are no overriding reasons why any future work that is valued should be of that kind and not some other. The wanted relationship is described through a projection whose reasonableness is assessed in ways similar to those used in other areas; for example, that the degree of discontinuity a new hypothesis presents is weighed against the probability that the account it provides will be both accurate and more comprehensive than the earlier ones. In the area under discussion, antecedent works not only redefine the candidate object by lending their support but are themselves reconstituted by accepting the candidate's offer of "new" characteristics for their own descriptions.

Were a candidate object to present itself through characteristics that largely duplicate those upon which the antecedent work's present value is based, little risk would be involved in granting support—but also little gain. In this case, the candidate would be predicting that the future work is valuable in much the same way the antecedent works *already* consider themselves to be valuable. The candidate, here, also gains least; for, by presenting its own description according to criteria already articulated, its own claim to value is compromised. It may be the case, for example, that if there are characteristics of the antecedent works, which are *not* presently valued but which *will be* consequential in a future work, the candidate, by not acknowledging them, loses value in later attributions.

But if a candidate presents itself in a mode that, to some given degree, is inimical to present values, then that presentation carries with it correlative degrees of risk and promise. The candidate may assert, for example, that the antecedent works are not adequately appreciated because they have *not (yet)* valued those characteristics the candidate is now ascribing to them. In this case, the concern of antecedent works would be with status *loss:* What confirmatory strength of accrued values would they risk losing by taking on an identity commensurate with the new characteristics? If the dislocations and the risks are too severe, the candidacy may well be rejected for another, more plausible one.

IV

Describing artworks through the "characteristics" or "properties" they possess is intuitively agreeable, and in this chapter, excepting the analysis in section II, I have stayed with this usage. However, as we know, the language of "predicate application" has certain advantages, one being a greater flexibility in moving between the "nature" of a thing and its "descriptions." As such flexibility is warranted—indeed, demanded—by my thesis, I continue the discussion by recasting "possession" into the terminology of "predication."

In the transactions that determine artistic status, judgments that characteristics are "like" or "unlike" each other play an important role. What are the criteria upon which such judgments are based? Is it simply a matter of which characteristics can "truly" be predicated of the entities involved? I do not believe so, for I hold that not every predicate that is true-of an object is also constitutive for it as an artwork; I also hold that not every one that is constitutive for it as an artwork under one interpretation is equally so under another. Many, although not all, of the predicate schemata comprising "every" interpretation overlap each other, but no one of these is completely contained within any other in any given interpretation. No interpretation affirms everything previously predicated by way of merely appending its own additions. The reorganization of a class of artworks, even as regards the weakest accepted candidate, entails discarding as well as adding predicates when we assess their adequacy, relative to each other, for the particular projection involved.[9]

I construe the predicate *W*, "———— is an artwork," to be coextensive with a large array of other predicates, both literal and metaphorical, that may variously speak to an object's mimetic probity or narrative power, to its mood or expressiveness, to its color, texture, and so on. Because I assume here that no predicate is totally inapplicable to an object (if it be only as a metaphor), I also assume that there is no predicate which, in principle, can be excluded from participating in an interpretation. However, this does not permit us to conclude that all such predicates participate in essentially the same way in each interpretation. To the contrary, the differences between two interpretations of an artwork can be accounted for through the patterns of exclusion and relative stress that organize the predicate schemata in each case. For example, although we cannot praise or criticize a work's expressiveness without changing our assessment *of* its overall value, we can nevertheless indicate, through the array of predicates we use, how much weight we give expressiveness *in* our assessment of its value. Such variability will hold between each and every predicate that applies at all.

Apropos the "same" extended entity, then, we can distinguish two relevant predicate schemata: The first ranges over all those objects to which we ascribe a particular constellation of properties; the second ranges over those objects that satisfy the transactional requirements for the term "art" as I outline them above. The relationship that holds between these predications is one of constant correlation between two unlimited sets. A given interpretation of an artwork requires a grading of the descriptive predicates that is consonant with the value claims that are being made. Such claims, as I have stated, are essentially predictions that identify *which* of the characteristics of the actual works should be regarded as constitutive in the light of anticipated value. As the attributing of artistic status is here held to be inseparable from a projection of anticipated value, it seems reasonable to suggest that those predicates not consonant with a given projection are discarded for that interpretation of the object as art. But new candidates for artistic status constantly appear, and no extant works, whatever their hesitations, are immune to the reinterpretations that these others bring with them. If this is so, then no description deemed inapplicable under any one interpretation is systematically excluded from any other. *Anything* an object expresses, for example, may be compatible with *some* interpretation of it as art, although *nothing* such an object may express is compatible with *every* interpretation of it as art.

V

Perhaps it would now be well (and welcomed) for me to leave this level of analysis and provide some examples of my theory as practice. I offer only one such example as my purpose here is methodological, not art-historical. What I have in mind is an account of alternatives in the interpretation of an artwork at the time of its candidacy. The work I select for this is a "difficult" one of Mondrian's middle period: the *Composition in Black and White* of 1917. I assume, for purposes of this discussion, that we are at the point in the attributing process when the conditions of candidacy are just being formulated, when the claims and counterclaims that would affirm or deny art status are being made. Here, I examine only a few of the many interpretations that could be made, but in doing so I take advantage of the fact that at least some "future works" from which this candidate might seek support are now part of our own "present." In section IV above, I define a future work for a given candidacy as theoretic or hypothetical. However, as I am now writing in the actual future of the work I have chosen, I refer only to actual works that are such as to fulfill *some* projection of a hypothetical future work at the time of my exampled work's candidacy. Of course, there is no compelling reason why, for this purpose, I should not evoke some work that is *as yet* unmade, but I want to show how some interpretations might actually work out.

Within the oeuvres of avant-garde artists, there are often works which, in retrospect, are seen to contain the germs of later achievements. But these

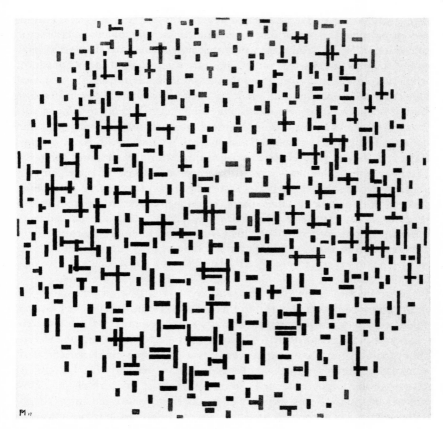

Piet Mondrian, *Composition in Black and White* (1917).
Oil on canvas, 39 × 39".
Collection, Rijksmuseum Kroller-Muller, Otterlo, Holland.

same works, at the time of their making, seem to have abandoned so much of what was then wanted for art—even of what the artist had previously done—that they are greeted with bewilderment and, often, rejection. The *White on White* of Malevich is surely one such work, as is the *Trois Demoiselles d'Avignon* of Picasso, and perhaps Kandinsky's first "pure abstraction" of 1910. There are, of course, many others. The work I discuss here, the *Composition in Black and White*, comes at the end of a series of works dating back to 1912 that are known, variously, as "Plus and Minus" or

"Pier and Ocean." I have a number of reasons for selecting this work. One of these is personal and comes out of memories when, as a student, I stared at (a reproduction of) this painting, wondering how anyone could possibly consider it to be art, and then became intrigued with the idea of a world in which people would take it as art. A second, less self-indulgent, reason is in my belief that this painting is still underappreciated, much as when it first appeared. But such lack of reception is not completely puzzling, for how *are* we to take this bare, symmetrical, colorless array of vertical and horizontal elements? Is it an artistic *reductio ad absurdum* which, once arrived at, signals a retreat to more "central" concerns through which discarded painterly luxuries can be reclaimed—now with greater assurance? Or is the painting a beginning, one that closes off its past and thrusts its own predecessors into history? Such questions, when filtered through my concern with the context of attributions, can be restated as follows: How would this painting, as a candidate, present itself? To which works would it apply in its quest for status, and what works would it evoke as support for its application? Of the many plausible scenarios that could be developed in answer here, I will consider only three.

The *Composition in Black and White* may be seen as an extreme statement of certain concerns found in the group of works known as "Pier and Ocean." Indeed, if we look at the painting in one way, we can see in it the spatial regression of a central vertical—much like a pier extending into the water. This vertical is not a shape, however; it is a "preferred configuration" that we make—or find—in the field of marks. Compatible with this illusionistic reading is the implied oval that acts as an internal "picture plane." This internal boundary keeps the painted marks from connecting with the external rectangle of the canvas edges and, in this way, militates against a frontal, "abstract," reading. Given the unwillingness of *this* version of candidacy to relinquish naturalistic illusion, what antecedent paintings could be applied to in the formation of a tradition class? Certainly, the "painterliness" of Mondrian's earlier versions of cubism (e.g., the "Tree Series") would be a pertinent value. Perhaps the late Cézanne watercolors could be subscribed to, and some Van Gogh drawings—even, to stretch a point, Courbet's seascapes of the 1860s. As this is a "conservative" version of candidacy, much of nineteenth-century preoccupation with nature and landscape could be brought in here. Turning to the other side of this candidacy, the evocation of a "future work," we find the situation to be more sparse. In Mondrian's own later paintings, the oval format appears a few times but is soon abandoned, and the theme becomes unremittingly abstract. A more supportive appeal, however, could be made to certain abstract-expressionist

paintings of the 1950s. In chapter 2, I discuss a possible "naturalistic" reading of Jackson Pollock's "field" paintings. This reading could also be made of
works of a later period, such as Philip Guston's *The Day* of 1964. Mondrian's
oval format is echoed in these works, for both Pollock and Guston also
"float" their images and thus avoid "fastening" them to the paintings'
edges. Of course, much else characteristic of these later works is unremarked
here: action, spontaneity, scale, and so on. This interpretation would also
seem to go against Mondrian's own theories, and against most critical accounts of his artistic evolution.

A second projection of a tradition class for this candidate comes closer to
standard accounts. This interpretation has as its themes the progressive
elimination of mimetic reference, the analytic reduction of "shape" into
"rhythm," and the expansion of pictorial elements into a larger environ-
mental matrix. The antecedent works appealed to here could also include the
Cézanne watercolors—but not for their understated elegance; rather, for the
structural "essences" they expose. Other antecedent works are closer at
hand: Picasso's analytic cubist works c. 1910, and Mondrian's own version
of analysis in the "Facade" paintings of the same period. The presentation
made here to these works would be that the progressive process of abstracting
is not to be "retreated from" (as Picasso can be said to have done) but to be
followed to its "logical" conclusion of a fully achieved abstraction. In this
sense, then, the *Composition in Black and White* is seen as Mondrian's first
"purely" abstract painting, the goal of his early efforts and the basis for his
later ones. Thus, when one seeks future works for this interpretation, they
can immediately be found in paintings Mondrian did shortly after this one—
such as *Composition in Blue B*—where lines and floating planes of color are
combined, the former rhythmically activating the latter's distribution.
When we pursue this emphasis on rhythm, and the concomitant rejection of
pictorial weight, we evoke the future of Mondrian's last work. In the *Victory
Boogie-Woogie* of 1943–44, the distinction between line and color disap-
pears, and the earlier oval format is redefined as a lozenge shape—a square
canvas stood on point. This is to be understood not as a quasi-mystical move
to enhance illusion but as a show of impatience with the confines of regular,
"passive" formats—a rejection of painting as a separate world reserved only
for appreciation. The picture plane is thus seen as an arbitrary limitation on
forms as they extend into, and activate, their surrounding spaces. Other
future works for this interpretation might be found in architecture, not so
much in the sculpted minimalism of, say, the Seagram Building but in the
functional-social complexes of Moshe Safdie's "Habitat," or Le Corbusier's
"Unité d'Habitation." Here the candidate's evocation is of an aesthetics of

rational relationships, which has applicability, as Mondrian himself indicates, within realms of architectural and communal planning. This is the "optimistic" version of the Hegelian "evolutionary thesis" that I discuss in chapter 1.

The third version of the candidacy of *Composition in Black and White* does not show the optimism of the second—or, perhaps, shows it in the sense that the values expressed there are inverted. In this interpretation, the move into purified realms of abstraction is affirmed, but the expansiveness and dynamics of application are denied. Pure form, here, becomes an occasion for contemplation, a solipsistic withdrawal into sameness. To find antecedent works within Mondrian's oeuvre, we must go back to the triptych *Evolution* of 1911, in which three symmetrical, stylized nudes suggest mystical—but not temporal—change; or perhaps to a *Chrysanthemum* of 1908, in which symmetry turns nature into an icon. However, it is of little use, here, to reach back into older art for antecedents; some can be found, of course—in medieval icons and so forth—but they do not really fit. This interpretation, of the three discussed, is historically the most discontinuous and self-conscious. The status of art is symbolized through stasis, not evolution. The integrity of the concept is maintained—but at the expense of its development. What is emphasized now in the *Composition in Black and White* is the symmetry that arrests and nullifies the part-whole origins of its naturalistic subject. This symmetry serves as a static formulation of the "reconciliation of opposites"—"positive-negative," "universal-particular," "matter-mind"—with which Mondrian's theosophical beliefs preoccupied him.[10] However, Mondrian's later paintings do not serve well here as future works, for they evidence a *process* articulation of these metaphysical opposites: The pictorial elements are brought into *asymmetrical* relationship in which tension replaces stasis as a means toward equilibrium. The search, then, for a future work must turn in other directions.

One such direction leads again to the work of Ad Reinhardt, which I discuss in chapter 2. Though a great admirer of Mondrian, Reinhardt was not a "process" Hegelian. His concept of abstraction is that of the unifying constancy underlying changes in style. The "minimalist" nature of twentieth-century abstraction, for this interpretation, is not so much evidence of "progress" in art as it is a waning of art's earlier social functions brought about by the usurpations of other forms in modern culture. These usurpations, however, are seen as welcome because they reveal the "timeless" values of art, and Mondrian is seen as the first to give these values an appropriate—impersonal and absolute—form.

There is another future work that may be plausible here, one that does not achieve stasis through an effort of withdrawal—as Reinhardt does—but presents repetition and monotony as perfectly natural states of affairs. I refer here to the works of Frank Stella, specifically to the *Marquis de Portago* of 1960. This painting, like Mondrian's *Composition in Black and White*, is linear, without color, and symmetrical. Unlike Reinhardt's paintings, there is no light, no emergence, no finality. "What one sees" and "what is there" are taken as mutually implicative—a theory of "nontheory."[11] As with Mondrian's adoption of the lozenge format, Stella's canvas is also "shaped"—but for a different reason. The shape he adopts—here, an indented rectangle—is but a consequence of the internal linear elements repeating outwardly, the last repetition defining the canvas edge. Thus, the pictorial elements are not "liberated" by the shape of the canvas; they are indistinguishable from it. The symmetry of this painting does have an iconic quality, but it also suggests a reference to the symmetries of everyday artifacts—a quality of "design." The passively mimetic nature of this reference belies Mondrian's belief in the transformative power of "pure plastic" relationships. In this, the Stella is socially conservative. Also, unlike Reinhardt's beliefs, Stella's work belies the value of maintaining the inviolateness of the category "art." Although this is, indeed, a version of art's social diffusion, it is so by virtue of art's symbolic default. The interpretation given above of the Stella painting as a future work of our candidacy, suggests a categorical boundary between avant-garde art and later, perhaps postmodernist, concerns.

VI

This concludes my discussion on the ontology of artworks, specifically, on the process by which something that aspires to the status of art achieves that status. I describe this process as an interpretation within an extended temporal context: the formation of a tradition class whose members are a group of antecedent works with which the candidate seeks to unite in a particular construal of historical style, and a group of future works whose projected existence is used as a justification for the formation of that class. As we have seen, there are many possible interpretations for any given candidacy, indeed, indefinitely many, for they arise out of our conjectures about what the future will be like, and these conjectures, in turn, influence the values we seek in things of our past.

The instability I ascribe to this process can be unsettling to the uses for which we ordinarily devise our theories. Of the three interpretations I sketch above, surely one is "preferable," more "correct" than the others. In a standard sense, this is true: Preferences are often hard come by, and correctness can be judiciously estimated. Yet we notoriously open our held preferences to critics for overturning—not because these preferences no longer reflect us but because, like old metaphors, they, and we, have become stale. Correctness, on the other hand, is often held to be independent of preference. No anxiety, for example, accompanies the thought that a preference might—and usually does—change. But an alternative to being correct is being incorrect, and we cannot rest here but must find a way to correctness again.

Avant-garde art often challenges our preferences by insisting that we must seek to understand—to be "correct about"—what is too unfamiliar for us to prefer. We often demand the assurance, within this challenge, that we will come to prefer what we learn to understand. I have called this the optimistic view, for it sees our preferences and our judgments as cumulatively joining in agreement over the course of time. I also consider this view conservative, for it does not require us to abandon either our past preferences or our past judgments: We need only to "build" upon them. I have described other views, however, that do not share this optimism, for they hold that our preferences act mainly to hinder our efforts toward understanding. The past is also seen here in a more "radical" way, as discontinuous with the present, merely providing us with cautions for our new formulations—information about what is henceforth to be avoided.

The various discussions of artworks throughout this book are all interpretations—in my sense of constructed tradition classes—and can thus be taken as examples supporting the theorizing in this last chapter. However, they do not offer alternatives, as do the examples discussed just above; they present single points of view, those which, admittedly, best conform to my own preferences—and my judgments.

Despite the changes in specific content from chapter to chapter, I do maintain emphasis on the "volatility" of the transactions through which I describe the realm of art. I take volatility to be a positive value for this realm, and I promote it by locating art in the intersection between work and theory—or, as in my title, between "art" and "concept." I hope, in this way, to insure that the endurance of art—a much overplayed virtue—is at least tempered by ongoing shifts in its descriptions. Some may find that my attempt to "speed up" this whole enterprise shows an antiinstitutional bias. I have no quarrel with institutions in their roles as codifiers and conservators. But we must also understand that to codify and conserve is itself an interpretation: only one way of relating artworks to some—not every—valued past and wanted future. As I have tried to show, there are other interpretations.

Now that the fear that art will die has largely abated, we are left with the unexpected burden of its future. Do my theories hold for the art about which I have uttered barely a word—the art of our "present" present? To answer this question, I must first answer another: What concepts could I find or fashion that would discriminate, out of everything presently "eligible," those things we wish to make intelligible as art? Once *this* were done, the rest could follow as it has in this book.

1 HEGEL, "PROGRESS," AND THE AVANT-GARDE IN EUROPE

1   Modern art is probably the historical period in art that is most extensively documented by its own contemporaries. This "self-consciousness" has often been proffered as a major characteristic of the period. In avant-garde art, as I define it here, a major theoretical component is found in the writings of the artists themselves. In addition to those I discuss—Mondrian, Kandinsky, and Klee—mention can be made of Breton, Gropius, Malevich, Gabo, Moholy-Nagy, the futurists, etc. Major non-avant-garde figures, such as Picasso and Matisse, are conspicuous in this regard for their avoidance of theoretical activity. For a comprehensive discussion of these issues, see Renato Poggioli, *The Theory of the Avant-Garde* (Cambridge: Harvard University Press, 1968).

2   Both Mondrian and Kandinsky were much influenced by theosophy, which can be considered a mystical offshoot of Hegelian historicism that stresses the evolution of "spirit" rather than culture.

3   G. F. W. Hegel, *Aesthetics*, trans. T. M. Knox (London: Oxford University Press [Clarendon Press], 1975), vol. 1, pp. 91–105.

4   This distinction can be substantiated by contrasting Kant's distinction between "theoretical" (teleological) ideas and "practical" ideas; cf. Immanuel Kant, "Idea for a Universal History," in *On History*, Library of Liberal Arts (New York: Bobbs-Merrill, 1967), pp. 11–26; and Hegel's account of the "realization of the idea of History" in *Reason in History*, Library of Liberal Arts (New York: Bobbs-Merrill, 1953), part 2, sec. 3.

5   G. F. W. Hegel, *Phenomenology of Mind*, Baillie translation (New York: Harper, 1967), sec. 8.

6   This argument is strongly made by Theodore Adorno in his *Philosophy of Modern Music*. See my discussion in chapter 3.

7   Hegel, *Aesthetics*, vol. 1, part 2, sec. 2, the classical ideal of a "spiritual-sensual" harmony.

8   A provocative discussion of this issue can be found in Arthur Danto, "The Last Work of Art: Artworks and Real Things," *Theoria* 39 (1973): 1–17, esp. part 4.

9   Hegel, *Aesthetics*, vol. 2. Hegel looks to past art for exemplars of all three divisions of his category of romantic art: The most plausible identification of his candidates seems to be, respectively, Raphael, Mozart, and Shakespeare. He actually speaks quite negatively about a contemporary composer who cannot be other than Beethoven. Whether this indicates a vocational inattention to current art activities or

a presentiment of art's "decline" is, of course, a speculative question—but an interesting one.

10   Allen Janik and Stephen Toulmin, *Wittgenstein's Vienna* (New York: Simon and Schuster, 1973), chap. 4.

11   This is a considerable claim, which I explore more fully in chapter 3 within the context of twelve-tone music. My basic point here is that the "alienation" associated with avant-garde art is not merely a disjunction in form between such works and the audience's aesthetic expectations but arises out of the demands a sympathetic appreciation would make on the audience's view of its own society.

12   Hegel, *Reason in History*, sec. 3.

13   Hegel, *Phenomenology*, chap. 7, sec. C.

14   Hegel, *Aesthetics*, vol. 2, part 3.

15   The *Gesamtkunstwerk* of Wagner might be seen as a banding together of the various arts as a way of bypassing their individual "inadequacies"—a sum that is greater than its parts. On a more egalitarian level, novel syntax in literature, the twelve-tone row and aleatory devices in music are some examples of "self-transcendence" within individual arts. The processes of abstraction and nonobjectivity, discussed in this chapter, are cases in point for the visual arts.

16   "Avant-garde" as both category designator and battlecry was unquestioned during the period under discussion—despite quarrels over membership and meaning. These days, of course, the use of the term is surrounded by perplexity—one reason why this chapter was written.

17   This topic has a vast literature, for the full elaboration of these changes would include everything we know as modern art. Here, the points made are introductory to the limited discussion of Mondrian and Kandinsky.

18   Although perspective developed gradually and with many variations, the "grand tradition" of usage can be located between Uccello and Tiepolo. Courbet is a bridge to modern art, as Giotto is a bridge to medieval art. "Preperspective" Western works and "nonperspective" Eastern works often show a "modern," episodic spatiotemporal structure.

19   One could argue that a work in any tradition is "formed" or "completed" through the act of scanning, and that the modern emphasis on process is merely a self-consciousness about means. Conversely, one could argue that this self-consciousness, refined, now permits us to "deconstruct" older works into contemporary ones. The claim I make for noncumulative scanning is that it does not presuppose either a thematic or a structural hierarchy in the work that is the subject of attention. This distinguishes it from a scanning in which such a characteristic is first identified and then discounted.

20   Randomness is indeed a virtue in certain modern movements, notably dada and, to some extent, surrealism. Its influences on later movements such as abstract expressionism and performance art are also considerable. This principle can be viewed as antihistoricist and, thus, as a (self-conscious) rejection of Hegelianism.

21   Premodern commentary, for the most part, assumes that Western art exhibits a progressive ability to present convincing illusions of the world: The encomiums

greeting Giotto's "naturalism" are a case in point. Modern commentary replaces this belief with that of value-neutral "conventions" of representation. Gombrich and Goodman—for all their quarrels—both theorize this second way. Some avant-garde theory, curiously, is closer to the older traditions but in a *converse* way, the preoccupation with trompe l'oeil techniques here being an earmark of *lesser* aesthetic value.

22   This claim can be found in Mondrian's writings as well as in those of the suprematists and constructivists.

23   Hegel, *Phenomenology*, pp. 229–40.

24   Walter Gropius, "My Conception of the Bauhaus Idea," in *50 Years Bauhaus*, Catalogue of Exhibition, Royal Academy of Arts (London, 1968), pp. 13–17.

25   Piet Mondrian, *Plastic Art and Pure Plastic Art* (1937; New York: Wittenborn, Schultz, 1947), pp. 10–15, 44–47, 50–53. It was not enough for Mondrian to rid his work of all vestiges of "natural appearances"; he also rejected the extensive lexicon of abstract shapes and combinations in favor of a minimal rectangle modified only by size, position and color. I suggest that one reason for this is Mondrian's wish to avoid the possibility of "anthropomorphism"—placing forms in a "narrative" relationship—that is suggested by shape variation.

26   Ibid., pp. 54, 58–60, 62.

27   Wassily Kandinsky, "On the Problem of Form" (1912), in *Theories of Modern Art*, ed. Herschel B. Chipp, (Berkeley: University of California Press, 1968), pp. 155–70.

28   Ibid., p. 168.

29   Paul Klee, "Creative Credo" (1920), in Chipp, *Theories of Modern Art*, pp. 183–84.

30   Kandinsky, "On the Problem of Form," p. 158. Kandinsky's criterion of inner necessity raises problems of the same sort as does Bell's "aesthetic emotion": It can only be operative through its "manifestation" in the formal characteristics of an artwork, yet the theory avoids making it causally dependent upon any particular set of formal characteristics. Indeed, the wanted claim here is that certain formal characteristics are valuable *because* they are produced through inner necessity. Inasmuch as Kandinsky—unlike Mondrian—refuses to fix the formal "syntax" for his aesthetic, he must rely on his sensibility's "private workings" to adjudicate among heterogeneous works. This poses few problems for artists and like-minded colleagues, some problems for critics, and considerable problems for aestheticians.

31   Ibid., p. 169.

32   Ibid., pp. 163–64, 167.

33   Ibid., p. 160.

34   Ibid., pp. 168–69.

2   KANT, ''FORM,'' AND THE AVANT-GARDE IN AMERICA

1   One historical juncture in the American schism between radical art and radical sociology is the exhibition mounted by the Museum of Modern Art in 1950 as

a protest against the character of the Metropolitan Museum annual of the same year. The exhibitors, then known as the "irascibles," included many of the major figures in abstract-expressionist art. Although this show was heralded as a triumph for the avant-garde, it also struck an "art for art's sake" theme which opposed the themes of artistic humanism and social responsibility dominating the other show. In a sense this occasion can be seen as a culmination of the dispute over the role of art that occurred within the WPA "Artist's Project" and the Federal Art Project throughout the 1930s. See Holger Cahill, "The Federal Art Project, 1936," in *Theories of Modern Art*, ed. Herschel B. Chipp (Berkeley: University of California Press, 1968), pp. 471–74.

2   See *Circle: International Survey of Constructivist Art* (New York: E. Weyhe, 1938). The articles in this (short-lived) periodical, written by major figures in the European avant-garde, range across the visual arts, architecture, planning, design, etc. They present an excellent cross-section of what I call European aesthetic utopianism.

3   See Clement Greenberg, "Modernist Painting" *Art and Literature*, Spring 1963.

4   See my discussion in chapter 6.

5   Immanuel Kant, *Critique of Judgment* (New York: Hafner Press, 1951). Compare the judgment of "taste" in the "Analytic of the Beautiful" with the function of "genius" in the "Analytic of the Sublime."

6   Ibid., p. 150.

7   See R. G. Collingwood's distinction between art and craft in *The Principles of Art* (New York: Oxford University Press, 1958), chap. 2.

8   We can wonder, in the context of twentieth-century art, what might correspond to the exclusivity of Kant's "genius." Perhaps it would be a judgment with Hegelian roots to the effect that, of all the creative and expressive issue of the new egalitarian aesthetic, only a few works will become "historically significant."

9   In Chipp, *Theories of Modern Art*, see Naum Gabo, "The Realist Manifesto," pp. 325–30; Piet Mondrian, "Plastic Art and Pure Plastic Art," pp. 349–62; Kasimir Malevich, "Suprematism," pp. 341–46.

10   See Clement Greenberg, *Art and Culture* (Boston: Beacon Press, 1961), esp. pp. 217–19.

11   The breakdown between artistic realms—e.g., between painting and theater —produces a kind of "antiart" art and is thus a legacy of the dada movement and of Marcel Duchamp. This does not become an important factor in American art until about 1960.

12   Greenberg, *Art and Culture*, pp. 133–38.

13   Barbara Rose, ed., *Art as Art: The Selected Writings of Ad Reinhardt* (New York: Viking Press, 1975), pp. 12–23.

14   This observation is based on a conversation I had with the painter Carl Holty in which he reminisced about Mondrian.

15   Rose, *Art as Art*, pp. 113–14.

16   Immanuel Kant, *Critique of Pure Reason* (New York: St. Martin's Press, 1965), p. 93.

3   ADORNO, ''PROTEST,'' AND THE TWELVE-TONE ROW

1   The text this commentary focuses on is Adorno's *Philosophy of Modern Music*. Although an early text, I believe it to be germinal in the formulation of his ideas on the development of music and the ''crisis'' of modernism. Adorno's application of the term ''modern'' is quite selective and excludes most early twentieth-century music. His correlation of ''modern'' with ''radical'' and his location of musical radicalism in ''dodecaphonic'' music, gives ''modern'' the same normative strength and limited range I associate, in chapter 1 and 2, with the term ''avant-garde.'' I trust, as we go on, that context will support the restricted sense.

2   The ''modern-traditional'' dichotomy, these days, seems oversimplified if not completely untenable. Although Adorno uses it, he takes pains to trace the (purely musical) continuity between nineteenth- and twentieth-century musical styles. Yet there seems no doubt that he also considers ''true modern''—dodecaphonic—music to be functionally of a different sort than its predecessors. As my purpose here is not to challenge this thesis but to trace some of its implications, I adopt this classification in my discussion. Traditional music in Adorno's usage refers primarily to classical and romantic music: the music of developing bourgeois cultures. Baroque music is some-what separate; its social context is that of autocracy, and in its polyphonic form it correlates more directly with modern music. Adorno divides contemporary music uncompromisingly between ''radical'' and ''decadent,'' prime exemplars of the latter being Stravinsky and late Hindemith. Such composers as Mahler and Křenek are transitional in his account to the major atonal composers: Schoenberg, Berg, and Webern. I do not comment here on Adorno's later involvement with such contemporaries as Stockhausen, Cage, and Boulez.

3   The term ''atonal'' can be misleading because, in a strict sense, all music is ''tonal,'' i.e., is an array of ''tones.'' Adorno uses the term to distinguish between music based upon the diatonic scale and music utilizing the twelve-tone row: dodecaphonic music. I follow this usage here.

4   The reference here is to Nelson Goodman's analysis in his *Languages of Art* (Indianapolis: Bobbs-Merrill, 1968), chap. 4.

5   G. F. W. Hegel, *Aesthetics*, trans. T. M. Knox (London: Oxford University Press [Clarendon Press], 1975), vol. 1, part 2.

6   I discuss this characteristic of avant-garde theory in chapter 1. In the writings of Kandinsky, Mondrian, and publications of the Bauhaus, we find the thesis that art has achieved a ''plateau'' of self-sufficiency which is the culmination of a historical development. Further development, on this account, entails the discovery and elaboration of possibilities inherent in this historical achievement but not a striving for further emancipation, the assumption being that there are—finally—no longer any restrictions to artistic freedom.

7   Theodor W. Adorno, *Philosophy of Modern Music*, trans. Anne G. Mitchell and Wesley V. Blomster (New York: Seabury Press, 1973), p. 130.

8   Ingratiation, as an auxiliary function of music, can be correlated with the concept of professionalism, i.e., the composer's undertaking a task identified by the larger

society as a desirable and needed one. The late romantic and modern turn to self-expression or newness as justifications for music-making undermines the notion of professionalism by discarding the criterion of social desirability. Adorno reinstates this criterion through his thesis of music's critical function. But, here, the perception of criticism as a social need issues not from the society in question but from a group that is alienated from its society.

9   In Plato's *Phaedrus* the lover "goes through" the attractions of physical beauty in order to advance to an appreciation of formal beauty. In that dialogue, sensual enjoyment is seen as revelatory rather than as inhibitory to the understanding of higher virtues. This is what is at issue here.

10   This argues against Collingwood's view on the matter.

11   In *Languages of Art*, Goodman makes the claim that differences between an original work and a "look-alike" forgery will eventually come to be noticed if one continues to look. Here, the importance of undiscerned notes in the context of traditional music is accounted for in a similar way. In both accounts, the possibility of eventual sensory discrimination is the consequent value for appreciation. I claim, however, apropos atonal music, that *non*discrimination constitutes a value.

12   Adorno, *Philosophy of Modern Music*, p. 84.

13   Ibid., p. 61.

13   Ibid., pp. 62, 63.

15   Ibid., p. 59.

16   To substantiate these claims, I enlisted the help of some composer friends who were willing to lead me through an analysis of four works: Schoenberg's Third Quartet, opus 30, and his Variations for Orchestra, opus 31; Webern's Piano Variations, opus 27, and his String Quartet, opus 28. I chose these works because Adorno's frequent references to them in *Philosophy of Modern Music* point to the notion of an inherent tension between row construction and sound; see pp. 73–74, with footnote, 83–84, 92, and 109–12. Although a measure-by-measure analysis is impractical here, I suggest that support for my claims would be found in one.

17   Adorno, *Philosophy of Modern Music*, p. 70.

18   Ibid., p. 42.

19   Ibid., pp. 39, 43.

20   Ibid., pp. 4, 9.

21   The examples here would be of such "transitional" composers as Mahler and Křenek as well as much of Berg's work, e.g., *Wozzeck*, and such early works of Schoenberg as *Erwartung*.

22   Adorno, *Philosophy of Modern Music*, pp. 20, 86.

23   Ibid., p. 27.

24   Adorno levels this accusation at Stravinsky and Hindemith, among others.

25   Adorno, *Philosophy of Modern Music*, p. 51.

26   Ibid., p. 125 n.

27   Ibid., pp. 124–27.

28   The phrase "art and experience" refers, of course, to John Dewey's book of that name. Dewey insists on a "public" aesthetic entity that is composed of both the

physical work and the experiences of it. In this refusal to give primacy to the epistemological question, Dewey shows his debt to Hegel. Adorno would not disagree with the desirability of Dewey's program; he would consider it a historical casualty.

29   Adorno, *Philosophy of Modern Music*, p. 124.

30   I discuss this issue at greater length in chapter 5.

4   "APPRECIATION," "OBLIGATION," AND AN ARTWORK'S END

1   In chapter 5 I describe another context in which artworks may be said to end—in that case through a question of what it means for a work to be "finished," a question of the artist's "provenance" over his own work.

2   This "incompatible-incommensurable" distinction is worked out in detail in Richard Rudner's "Show or Tell: Incoherence among Symbol Systems," *Erkentniss* 12 (1978): 129–51.

3   The reference here is to George Dickie's thesis that the status "artwork" is consequent on an "agent-of-the-artworld." I take this up at some length in chapters 5 and 6.

4   I remember seeing such a piece at the Whitney Museum a number of years ago, but I have not been able to find out the exact date or the artist's name. My intention here is not to be critical of the piece but only to point out that its extraartistic (artifactual) identity poses no challenge to its status as art.

5   In *Languages of Art* (Indianapolis: Bobbs-Merrill, 1968), Nelson Goodman limits his criterion of "history of production" to the constitutivity of autographic works. I use it here, somewhat altered, in reference to film which, in Goodman's system, seems most readily classified as an allographic form. However, my concern with the factor of intentions (one that Goodman explicitly rejects) leads me to this special usage.

6   The classic argument against "intentions" as determinants of works is found in W. K. Wimsatt, Jr., and Monroe Beardsley, "The Intentional Fallacy," in *The Verbal Icon*, ed. W. K. Wimsatt, Jr. (Lexington: University of Kentucky Press, 1954), chap. 1.

7   The "intentional fallacy" is much too formidable an edifice for me to tackle in any detail here—although I have serious doubts about it. I suspect that intentions, assertions of them as well as other evidence—even conjectures about them—are all properly constitutive in how we know artworks. I do deny, however, that intentions are privileged factors in, or grounds for, such knowledge.

8   I discuss the relationship between "status" and "value" in detail in chapter 6.

5   ARTWORKS THAT END AND OBJECTS THAT ENDURE

1   George Dickie, *Art and the Aesthetic: An Institutional Analysis* (Ithaca, N.Y.: Cornell University Press, 1974), chap. 1. I have some quarrels with the form of Dickie's analysis, which I take up in chapter 6.

2   Arthur Danto, "The Artworld," *Journal of Philosophy* 63 (1964): 580.

3   George Dickie, "A Response to Cohen: The Actuality of Art," in *Aesthetics*, ed. G. Dickie and R. Sclafani (New York: St. Martin's Press, 1977), p. 200.

4   Nelson Goodman, *Languages of Art* (Indianapolis: Bobbs-Merrill, 1968), chap. 5.

5   Joseph Margolis, *Art and Philosophy* (Atlantic Highlands, N.J.: Humanities Press, 1980), pp. 2, 21–22.

6   Ibid.

7   Dickie, *Art and the Aesthetic*, chap. 1.

8   Let us take W/O to stand for "work/object," and a for "begins before," m for "coincides with," z for "endures beyond." We can specify one "beginnings-ends" relationship as follows: Wmm/Omm. This states that the beginnings and ends of both work and object coincide. Another relationship is $Wa\text{-}/O\text{-}z$. This states that the work begins before the object, and the object endures beyond the work. The nine variations I identify are: Wmm/Omm, $Wm\text{-}/Omz$, $Wmz/Om\text{-}$, $Wam/O\text{-}m$, $W\text{-}m/Oam$, $W\text{-}z/Oa\text{-}$, $Wa\text{-}/O\text{-}z$, $Waz/O\text{-}\text{-}$, $W\text{-}\text{-}/Oaz$. I do not include such contradictory specifications as Waz/Oaz, which states that both work and object begin before each other and endure beyond each other.

9   S. H. Butcher, *Artistotle's Theory of Poetry and Fine Art*, 4th ed. (New York: Dover, 1951), p. 27.

10   The reference here is to an incident in Rome in which an artist, for whatever reasons, damaged the *Pietà* with a hammer. The sculpture has since been restored.

11   George Dickie makes this type of distinction between "status" and "value" attributions. I argue against his thesis in chapter 6.

12   I distinguish here between "aesthetic" and "legal" rights, e.g., between rights based upon authorship and rights based upon ownership. The rights of ownership can legally deny to the author (artist) the exercise of certain aesthetic rights, e.g., repainting his painting when it is owned by another. Ownership, as such, seems not to carry aesthetic rights. The matter becomes complex when the question is asked whether aesthetic rights can limit legal rights; e.g., are there situations where the right to destroy a legally owned work can (should) be denied? One of my concerns, here, is with the relationship between such conflicting rights and the status of artwork.

13   Goodman, *Languages of Art*, chap. 5.

14   I distinguish here between the terms "theoretic" and "theoretical." My "theoretic work" is construed as an actual, (indirectly) discriminable, entity. I reject the term "theoretical" because of such connotations as "possible" or "fictional."

15   Margolis, *Art and Philosophy*, chaps. 2–3.

16   Joseph Margolis, *Persons and Minds* (Dordrecht: D. Reidel, 1978).

17   I first broached these concerns in my dissertation: "The Attribution of 'Art' to Objects" (Ph.D. diss., Washington University, St. Louis, 1977).

6   A BASIS FOR ATTRIBUTIONS OF ''ART''

1   Arthur Danto, "The Artworld," *Journal of Philosophy* 63 (1964): 571–84.

2   George Dickie, *Art and the Aesthetic: An Institutional Analysis* (Ithaca, N.Y.: Cornell University Press, 1974), pp. 34–52.

3   Monroe Beardsley makes a strong case for the thesis that artworks exhibit their constitutive characteristics. As I interpret him, Beardsley does not deny the import of other, nonexhibited, characteristics in determinations of art, but he does consider the exhibited set to constitute a necessary condition for art status. (Monroe Beardsley, *Aesthetics* [New York: Harcourt-Brace, 1958], particularly chap. 6.)

4   Arthur Danto, "Artworks and Real Things," *Theoria* 39 (1973): 78–79.

5   Ted Cohen, "The Possibility of Art: Remarks on a Proposal by Dickie," *Philosophical Review* 82 (1973): 78–79.

6   George Dickie, "A Response to Cohen: The Actuality of Art," in *Aesthetics*, ed. G. Dickie and R. Sclafani (New York: St. Martin's Press, 1977), p. 200.

7   George Dickie, *Aesthetics* (Indianapolis: Bobbs-Merrill, 1971), chap. 11.

8   Richard Sclafani, "Artworks, Art Theory, and the Artworld," *Theoria* 39 (1973): 19–34.

9   Danto holds that new predicates appropriate to artworks are added to the extant aggregate of "artistically relevant" predicates by radical candidates ("The Artworld," pp. 582–84). He does not indicate that any predicates which are once true-of artworks (K [relevant] predicates that are f) can subsequently be discarded. His concept of art status, then, is like that of christening—once attained, it is irrevocable. I feel that such a status is more precarious and, indeed, can be lost to an object in the case that no agent (or theory) any longer affirms it as a work. (See chapter 5, herein.)

10   "Note 6" from Mondrian's "Notebooks" of 1914, in *Piet Mondrian*, ed. Michel Seuphor (New York: Abrams, 1956), pp. 117–18.

11   Frank Stella, in *Readings in American Art since 1900*, ed. Barbara Rose (New York: Praeger, 1968), p. 179.

INDEX

Abstract expressionism, 30, 38, 62
Academy, 4, 38
Adorno, Theodor, 5, 45–60, 119–21
Aesthetic, 5, 28; vs. artistic, 5, 67–69;
   vs. nonaesthetic, 61–67; rights, 83–87,
   122; utopianism, 30, 118
Alienation, 6, 46, 50
Appreciation, 5, 32–34; in music, 50–56;
   vs. obligation, 61–75
Architectonic, 19
Architecture as "symbolic" art, 16
Aristotle, *Poetics*, 80, 122
Art: abstract, 5, 10, 20–28, 106–11; as art,
   42, 73, 74; candidate for status of,
   92–113; classificatory sense of, 7, 95–96;
   evaluative sense of, 7, 95–96; limits of, 7;
   modern, 9, 10, 35, 59; predications of,
   96–99, 104–6; transactional theory of,
   101–6
Art work: as antecedent, candidate, future
   work, 7, 90, 101–11; as artifact, 95, 97;
   concrete vs. theoretic, 89–91; didactic
   function of, 64; end of, 61–75, 76–91;
   finished vs. unfinished, 83–91; image in,
   64, 71, 72; as non-appreciable, 67–69,
   72–74; status of, 76–91, 92–113
Artworld, 67, 76; agent of, 92–113
Avant-garde, 3–6, 93, 106, 112, 115;
   American phase, 29–44; European phase,
   29–44; in music, 45–60

Bauhaus, 26, 117, 119
Beardsley, Monroe, 94, 121, 123
Beauty, 13, 32
Beethoven, Ludwig van, 46, 50; *Eroica*, 84,
   115
Bell, Clive, 117

Benjamin, Walter, 58
Berg, Alban, 5, 46, 119, 120
Boulez, Pierre, 119
Bourgeois, 2, 46, 50
Brahms, Johannes, 46
Breton, André, 115
Butcher, S. H., 122

Cage, John, 119
Cahill, Holger, 118
Cézanne, Paul, 108
Characteristic, 27, 28
Chipp, Herschel, 118
*Circle: International Survey of Construc-
   tivist Art*, 118
Cohen, Ted, 123
Collective, 14, 18, 20
Collingwood, R. G., 118
Composition, 40
Concept, 3, 32, 36–40
Conceptual linkage, 3, 32, 35, 36, 44, 59, 63
Connoisseur, 63, 64, 66
Constructivism, 38
Contextual thesis, 7, 92–94
Convention, 31
Corbusier, Le, "Unité d'Habitation," 109
Courbet, Gustave, 19, 108, 116
Creativity, 35–37
Cubism, 23
Cultural criticism, 13, 21, 29, 30
Culture, 11–14

Dada, 41, 77, 118
Danto, Arthur, 7, 76, 92, 94, 121, 123
Decadence, 13
de Kooning, Willem, 42
Denial, 37–40